The Marriage License Bonds

of
Lancaster County, Virginia
from
1701 to 1848

Stratton Nottingham

Please direct all correspondence and orders to:

www.southernhistoricalpress.com
or
SOUTHERN HISTORICAL PRESS, Inc.
PO BOX 1267
375 West Broad Street
Greenville, SC   29601
southernhistoricalpress@gmail.com

Originally published: Onanock, VA. 1927
Reprinted: Southern Historical Press, Inc.
Greenville, SC 2017
ISBN #0-89308-867-6
Printed in the United States of America

Alderson, John m. Rachel Davenport 31 Jan 1787
Thaddeus Pope sec.

Alexander, Angus m. Betsey T. Pollard 20 Nov 1797
Peter Tankersley sec.

Alfred, Robert m. Jane Mitchell 1 Apr 1839, Thomas
Brown sec.

Alfred, Samuel m. Nancy Schofield 2 Sept 1802
James Towles sec.

Alford, Abel m. Janette W. Wallace 15 May 1823
Jasper Stott sec.

Alford, John m. Patty Jones 18 Jan 1806, James
Towles sec.

Alford, John m. Elizabeth Gundrey 18 Jan 1832
John Gundrey sec.

Alford, Nathan m. Nancy Bell 8 Feb 1811, J. Towles
sec.

Alford, Nathan m. Nancy Wilkerson 3 Aug 1824
Benjamin M. Walker sec.

Alford, Samuel m. Frances Coates 4 July 1810
Thomas Carter sec.

Allison, John of Prince George County m. Frances
Hill Currie 28 Nov 1796 Elizabeth
Currie sec.

Allen, Reubin m. Hannah Bailey 15 Dec 1775, John
Bailey sec.

Allen, William m. Elizabeth Cox wid. 12 Dec 1798
James Towles sec.

Anderson, Henry E. m. Frances L. McTyre 31 Jan
1825, John McTyre sec.

Angell, Baker m. Sarah Chilton 21 Dec 1786,
Joseph Hickerson sec.

Angel, John m. Betsey Isles 8 Oct 1801 James
Towles sec.

Angel, Samuel m. Mary West 7 Mar 1832, John Komm
sec.

Arms, Walter m. Nancy Harding 7 May 1804, Elias
Hazard sec.

Arms, Walter m. Betsey O. Tarklison 21 Dec 1807
Alexander Marsh sec.

Ashbury, Joel D. m. Mary Jane Hinton 22 Feb 1844
Anthony M. Sanders sec.

Ashburne, George m. Judith Dodson 2 Dec 1802
Charles Dodson, Jr. sec.

Ashburne, James m. Sally Davis Taylor 4 July 1812
Thomas Currell sec.

Ashburne, Luke m. Elisabeth Wheeler 6 Jan 1787
William Barber sec.

Ashbourn, Griffin m. Lilly Walker 22 Mar 1815
Fleet Cox sec.

Ashbourne, Luke m. Susanna Roberts, dau John Roberts
     9 July 1800, Michael Wilder sec.

Ashbourn, William G. m. Lucy Hughlett 2 May 1837
     Isaac Pitman sec.

Ashbourn, William m. Sally Walker 18 May 1841 John
     Ford sec.

Atwell, Thomas T. m. Polly J. Palmer 21 July 1823
     John Thrift sec.

Bailey, Charles m. Mary Chowning Dunaway dau.
     Samuel & Nancy Dunaway, born Mar 18
     1781, 2 Apr 1802, John Chowning Jr. sec.

Bailey, Charles m. Esther Brown 28 Sept 1814
     Thomas Shearman sec.

Bailey, Hugh m. Frances Chowning 8 Jan 1798/9
     William Chowning sec.

Bailey, Hugh m. Salley M. Shearman 18 May 1801
     Thomas Shearman sec.

Bailey, John m. Judith Brent 17 June 1765, Hugh
     Brent sec.

Bailey, Jessee m. Lucy Carter 18 Oct 1804, James
     Robb sec.

Ballendine, William m. Mary Ann Ewell, wid. 16
     Oct 1724, Thomas Edwards sec.

Ball, Cyrus m. Fidelia Downman, dau. R.W.Downman
     2 Nov 1807, Joseph Ball Downman sec.

Ball, David m. Ellen Heale dau. George Heale, 29
     May 1727, George Heale sec.

Ball, George m. Judith Payne 10 Oct 1735,
     Merriman Payne sec.

Ball, George, Jr. of Northumberland County m.
     Anna Taylor, dau. Elizabeth Taylor,
     14 June 1736, Thomas Edwards sec.

Ball, Hilkiah m. Hannah Ball dau. Sarah E.Ball
     2 Aug 1819, Joseph Ball, Jr. sec.

Ball, Hilkiah m. Sarah E. Simmonds 15 Nov 1845
     Thomas Brent sec.

Ball, Jesse m. Agatha Conway 9 Mar 1765/6 Edwin
     Conway sec.

Ball, Jesse C. m. Peggy Mitchell 17 Feb 1789/90
     Rich: Mitchell sec.

Ball, John m. Mary Ball dau. Lettice Ball 12 Mar
     1765/6, Mungo Harvey sec.

Ball, John B. m. Catherine E. Montague, dau. Lewis
     B. Montague 13 Apr 1846, Robert J.
     Mitchell sec.

Ball, John G. m. Elizabeth T. Payne 24 Jan 1822
     John Payne sec.

Ball, John S. m. Nancy Opie 8 Apr 1799 Thomas
    Taylor sec.

Ball, James Wallace m. Anne Ball 31 May 1779
    Richard Selden sec.

Ball, Joseph, widower, m. Ann Canell 25 Jan 1797
    George Ball sec.

Ball, Luke m. Rebecca Hudnall Haynie, dau. Hancock
    Haynie 1 Jan 1835, William Haydon sec.

Ball, Spencer m. Ann Ball Robertson, dau. Ann
    Robertson 12 Apr 1799, Robert M. Robertson sec.

Ball, Samuel m. Anne Taylor 25 Nov 1717, Arthur
    Clark sec.

Ball, William, Jr. m. Margaret Ball, dau. Richard
    Ball, 6 Feb. 1723, David Ball sec.

Bannerman, Mark of Middlesex County m. Catherine
    Barker 12 Aug 1724, William Payne sec.

Barnett, John m. Molly Haydon, dau. Lucy Haydon
    11 Feb 1811, Griffin Haydon sec.

Barnett, Joseph m. Polly George 11 July 1836, James
    Ingram sec.

Barrett, George m. Ann Haynie 22 Oct 1784, Thomas
    Pollard sec.

Barrett, William C. of Northumberland County m.
    Cephronia George 20 Dec 1847, Robert T.
    Dunaway sec.

Barrock, Griffin m. Elizabeth Newby 14 Nov 1832
    Richard Hackney sec.

Barrock, Newby m. Nancy Payne dau. Edward Payne
    22 Dec 1814, William S. Doggett sec.

Barrock, William m. Lucy Dunaway 23 Nov 1813, James
    Towles sec.

Barrick, William m. Nancy Weymoth 16 June 1821
    Benjamin Walker sec.

Basye, Elismond m. Betsy Candiff 27 Aug 1793 John
    Chilton sec.

Basye, Thomas m. Eugenia Carter 20 Nov 1848, John
    B. Bramham sec.

Batten, William m. Botty Pollard 1 July 1771
    Thomas Stott sec.

Beale, Alford of Richmond County m. Millan Downman
    13 June 1810, Joseph B. Downman sec.

Beale, Henry, Jr. m. Susan R. Robinson 6 Feb 1839
    James Robinson sec.

Beale, John Eustace m. Elizabeth Lee, dau. Charles
    Lee, 5 Mar 1771, Richard B. Lee sec.

Beale, Robert m. Elizabeth N. Robinson 26 Feb. 1844
    James Robinson sec.

Beale, Thomas of Richmond County m. Jane Currie
    dau. David Currie 10 July 1764, Leroy
    Griffin sec.

Beacham, Joseph H. m. Sarah M. C. Gresham 13 Aug
    1834, John Gresham sec.

Beane, Armistead m. Amy Weaver 3 Mar 1810, Oliver
    Towles sec.

Beane, Edward (signed "Bain") m. Ann P. Lunsford
    1 Dec 1828, George T. Beane sec.

Beane, Edwin m. Elizabeth Edwards 27 Dec 1790
    John Beane, Jr. sec.

Bean, George, Jr. m. Polly Warren, dau. William
    Warren, 11 Oct 1788, Richard Pitman sec.

Bean, George m. Fanny Sebree 18 Jan 1809, Thomas
    Beane, Jr. sec.

Beane, George E. m. Elizabeth L. Biscoe 14 Jan
    1825, John Hutchings sec.

Beane, John m. Armon George 31 Dec 1823, Wickliff
    George sec.

Beane, John M. m. Catherine Beane 23 Jan 1826
    Johnson Beane sec.

Beane, Leroy m. Margaret Ann Taff 2 Jan 1843
    Thomas Taff sec.

Bean, Peter m. Catherine Pollard 5 Nov 1786, Abner
    Palmer sec.

Beane, Peter m. Betty Mott 9 Nov 1799, William
    George sec.

Beane, Peter, Jr. m. Elizabeth C. Lawson, dau.
    Henry C. Lawson, 25 Oct 1815, John Edmonds
    sec.

Beane, Peter H. m. Frances M. Stott 13 May 1834
    Archibald Hinton sec.

Beane, Robert E. m. Mary Biscoe Towell, dau. Mark
    Towell 18 Nov 1817, Charles Yerby sec.

Beane, Richard T. m. Agnes C. Talley 13 Feb 1841
    George R. Talley sec.

Beane, Silas m. Milley Cundiff 6 Oct 1831, William
    C. Callahan sec.

Beane, Thomas m. Ellen Owen 2 Nov 1806, Giles
    Eubank sec.

Beane, Thomas J. m. Mary B. Beane 23 Apr 1831
    Thomas James, Jr. sec.

Beane, Warner m. Elizabeth C. Buchan 18 Nov 1839
    Nicholas P. Buchan sec.

Beane, William m. Sally Forrester 16 Dec 1839
    Richard Pitman sec.

Beane, William J., son of Frances Beane, m. Juliet
    C. Boothe, 21 June 1843, Henry Boswell sec.

Bell, Coleman m. Agga Weaver 26 Dec 1806, Nathan
  Alford sec.

Bell, John m. Franckey Edmonds 15 July 1740, Ezekiel
  Gilbart sec.

Bell, James L. m. Hannah M. Shearman 10 July 1833
  James W. Degges sec.

Bee, William m. Sealyer Nickings 1 Jan 1847, John
  Kelly sec.

Bennett, John m. Dolly Sampson 26 Mar 1808, Ezekiel
  Haydon sec.

Bennett, Richard of Westmoreland County m. Catherine
  Lawson, dau. Thomas Lawson, 28 Oct 1793
  Thomas Lawson sec.

Berry, George m. Jane Carter 16 -- 1783, John
  Lunsford sec.

Berrick, Griffin m. Eliza B. Flowers 4 July 1843,
  Richard Coleman sec.

Betts, Royster, Sr. m. Catherine Watts 5 Dec 1831
  Ewell Watts sec.

Biscoe, Henry L. m. Sarah C. Blakemore 15 Dec 1834
  Thomas C. Callahan sec.

Biscoe, Robert m. Elizabeth Lawson d. Henry Lawson
  31 May 1727, Thomas Edwards sec.

Biscoe, Robert m. Nancy Beane 18 Dec 1815, William
  T. Yerby sec.

Biscoe, William m. Hannah Blakemore 2 Dec 1780
  Edward Blakemore sec.

Blakey, Robert L. m. Elizabeth A. Rogers, 4 July
  1842, William H. Kirk sec.

Blackmore, Edward m. Hannah Stevens 11 Sept 1747
  Thomas Pollard sec.

Blackmore, Edward m. J---Neasum 9 Nov 1750, Gavin
  Lowry sec.

Blakemore, Edward m. Betty Rogers 8 May 1778, John
  Chowning sec.

Blakemore, William m. Tomza Chowning 29 Nov 1801
  James Towles sec.

Blakemore, William C. m. Lilly T. Thrall 28 Oct 1830
  John Chowning sec.

Bland, Francis ("Blane" in body of bond) m. Elizabeth
  Hughs 28 Nov 1830, Henry L. McNamara sec.

Bland, Theodoric m. Ann Pollard 8 June 1811, James
  Pollard sec.

Blin, Charles m. Judith Edwards 16 Nov 1780, John
  Blin sec.

Blinco, John m. Mary Connelly dau. George Connelly
  14 June 1759, John Connolly sec.

Bluefoot, William m. Margaret Jones, dau. Sally Jones
  28 May 1846, Opie Jones sec.

Boatman, John m. Nancy Mason 15 Jan 1798, James
        Doggett sec.
Boatman, John m. Judith Gundry 20 Oct 1824, Thomas
        P. Hill sec.
Boatman, John D. m. Margaret C. K. Percifull, dau.
        Margaret Percifull, 19 Aug 1833, Fleet
        Self sec.
Boatman, William m. Bridget Brinin 1 July 1771
        Peter Reveer
Boatman, William m. Sarah Yerby 18 Jan 1781
        Thomas Pollard sec.
Bonawell, Reubin m. Grace Wallace 15 Dec 1794
        William Wallace sec.
Bond, John m. Sarah Sharpe 22 June 1753, George
        Wale sec.
Bond, Thomas m. Kitty Hill 14 June 1804, James
        Towles sec.
Booth, Obadiah m. Frances Davis 17 Jan 1799
        William Newby sec.
Booth, William P. m. Frances Mitchell 26 Dec 1826
        John C. Booth sec.
Boss, John m. Mary Degge 10 Mar 1764, Charles
        Lee sec.
Bottoms, Thomas m. Hannah Cox 25 June 1800, George
        Dameron, Jr. sec.
Bottoms, James m. Jane Miller 18 Jan 1841, James
        Miller sec.
Bowles, Benjamin m. Charlotte Harris 20 June 1795
        Joseph Carter, Jr. sec.
Boyd, David m. Leannah Hutchings 20 Mar 1833
        Joseph D. Pursell sec.
Boyd, John m. Margaret Dunaway 19 Feb 1729, George
        W. Dunaway sec.
Boyd, Robert m. Nancy Pitman 2 June 1791, James
        Pitman sec.
Boyd, Royston C. m. Mary Marsh 25 Mar 1808
        George James sec.
Boyd, Thomas m. Elizabeth H. George 1 Jan 1831
        John Beane sec.
Boyd, Thomas m. Lucy Wheeler 10 Dec 1833, William
        Boyd sec.
Boyd, William m. Ann Kirkham 15 July 1833
        Braxton Kirkham sec.
Braxton, George, Jr. m. Mary Carter, sister of
        John Carter - Consent of John Carter
        dated 16 Jan 1732/3

Bradley, John m. Elizabeth Alfred, dau. Robert & Margaret Alfred 2 Apr 1800, James Towles sec.

Bradley, William m. Dorinda Galloway 21 Mar 1825 Hiram Chilton sec.

Bradley, William m. Caroline B. Stimson 25 Apr 1843 James Tally sec.

Bramham, John B. m. Priscilla Downman 14 Mar 1835 William Jones, sec.

Bramham, John B. m. Margaret E. Y. Carter 19 Oct 1840, A. L. Carter sec.

Bradberry, James m. Peggy Dodson, dau. Charles Dodson, 19 Sept 1808, James Riveer sec.

Bradbury, William m. Elizabeth McTyre 6 Dec 1811 Edward Payne sec.

Brest, Hugh m. Easter Shearman -- Oct 1761 Rowleigh Shearman sec.

Brent, Charles m. Catherine Kirk -- Dec 1791 Anthony Kirk sec.

Brent, Charles S. m. Sally H. McTyre 18 July 1825 Armistead J. Palmer sec.

Brent, Elias B. m. Elizabeth Edwards 31 Mar 1824 Charles H. Leland sec.

Brent, George m. Joanna Wale 17 Dec 1772, William Griggs sec.

Brent, George m. Sarah Ann Simmons 15 Jan 1784 Martin Shearman sec.

Brent, George m. Sarah Edmunds dau. Elias Edmunds 18 Feb 1792, Anthony Kirk sec.

Brent, George, Jr. m. Catherine Tapscott 29 Aug 1816, William F. Yerby sec.

Brent, Hugh m. Susannah Payne, dau. George Payne 6 Sept 1750, Anthony Sydnor sec.

Brent, Hugh m. Mary T. Lawson 7 Jan 1796, Joseph Stephens sec.

Brent, Isaac m. Mary Ann Dameron 8 Mar 1819, James Towles sec.

Brent, Jonathan m. Molly Brent 15 Sept 1799 Vincent Brent sec.

Brent, John m. Judith Norris, wid. 1 Apr 1791 Charles Brent sec.

Brent, John, widower, m. Ann Deggs 8 June 1796 William Brown sec.

Brent, James m. Sarah Cammell 4 Oct 1768, Coleman Doggett sec.

Brent, James m. Elizabeth Hunt 25 May 1780 William Lawson sec.

Brent, James m. Frances Hunton 17 June 1805, John
    Gibson sec.

Brent, James D. m. Fanny Brent 16 Jan 1809 Thomas
    James sec.

Brent, James, Jr. m. Ann S. Brent 24 Mar 1814
    Isaac Brent sec.

Brent, James m. Elizabeth L. Dameron 2 July 1819
    George Brent sec.

Brent, James K. m. Lucy C. Garlington 27 July 1821
    William H. Brent sec.

Brent, James m. Mary Wright 18 Feb 1834, William
    Brent sec.

Brent, Kenner m. Elizabeth Brent 29 Jan 1816,
    George Brent sec.

Brent, Martin m. Ann Chilton 29 Dec 1796, Joseph
    Stephens sec.

Brent, Maurice m. Lucy Flower 16 July 1764, Hugh
    Brent sec.

Brent, Newton m. Ann Stepto Lawson 14 Apr 1779
    John Berryman sec.

Brent, Richard W. H. m. Sally M. Gibson 15 Jan
    1833, James Harding sec.

Brent, Thomas m. Judith King, wid. 20 Oct 1774
    William Boatman sec.

Brent, Thomas m. Lucy Brent 18 Feb 1779, John
    Clayton sec.

Brent, Vincent m. Margaret S. Lawson 24 June 1786
    Thomas N. Lawson sec.

Brent, William m. Lisha Wale 9 Aug 1734 John
    Wale sec.

Brent, William m. Judith King, wid. 11 May 1753
    William Carter sec.

Brent, William m. Elliner Stott 20 May 1779
    William Carpenter sec.

Brent, William m. Elizabeth L. Hall 19 Aug 1809
    James Brent sec.

Brent, William H. m. Catherine M. Carter 20 Nov
    1823, Elias E. Brent sec.

Bridgman, William m. Jane N. Hunt 17 Dec 1825
    Robert Smither sec.

Briscoe, George m. Patty Potts dau. Thomas Potts
    Thomas Potts sec.

Briscoe, John m. Jane Carpenter 16 Dec 1811,
    John Carpenter sec.

Briscoe, Thomas m. Katherine Payne 7 Sept 1812,
    William Payne sec.

Bristow, James m. Agatha Mitchell 17 Feb. 1758
    Robert Mitchell sec.

Bristow, Larkin S. m. Catherine Seward 15 Dec 1828
      John Chowning sec.

Brown, Burges m. Molly Mason 31 Dec 1807, Frizzell
      McTyre sec.

Brown, Charles L. m. Maria J. Payne 4 Apr 1836
      Benjamin Waddey sec.

Brown, John m. Elizabeth James 2 July 1722, Thomas
      Purcell sec

Brown, John m. Elizabeth Mason 23 May 1786, James
      Yerby sec.

Brown, John m. Elizabeth Robinson 28 Sept 1843
      Cyrus Robinson sec.

Brown, James W. m. Priscilla Kent 13 Dec 1836
      Cyrus Hazard sec.

Brown, Rawleigh m. Nancy Robinson 17 Dec 1817
      Moses Robinson sec.

Brown, Rawleigh W. m. Ann H. George 16 Apr 1846
      E. G. Shearman sec.

Brown, Robert m. Nancy Dunaway 19 July 1837,
      Francis Sebree sec.

Brown, Spencer m. Judith Payne 17 May 1802 Thomas
      Shelton sec.

Brown, Thomas m. Elizabeth G. Lee 20 Oct 1807
      James Towles sec.

Brown, Vincent m. Juliett Ann Connolly 19 Dec 1838
      William C. Connolly sec.

Brown, Washington O. m. Mary Susan Walker 11 Mar
      1846, Lewis H. Dix sec.

Brown, William m. Judith Clayton 24 Jan 1793, John
      K. Schofield sec.

Brown, William, widower m. Peggy Haydon, wid. 19
      Dec 1796, Charles Lee sec.

Brown, William m. Betsey Coats 16 Jan 1804
      Rawleigh Coats sec.

Brown, William m. Sally Pitman, wid. 20 Feb. 1804
      Nathan Spriggs sec.

Brown, William m. Siller G. Stott 24 June 1815
      James Brent sec.

Brown, William m. Susan Coats 1 Jan 1817, Thomas
      Coats sec.

Brown, William m. Catherine Garner 29 Mar 1829
      Robert Mitchell sec.

Brown, William W. m. Jane Hunton, dau. Susan
      Hunton 8 Apr 1831, Kendall Lee sec.

Brosier, Joseph m. Mary Harris 8 Mar 1726
      Richard Chichister sec.

Brockenbrough, Newman of Richmond County m. Sarah
      Heale 24 Oct 1715, Austin Brockenbrough
      sec.

Brumley, Daniel m. Susanna Holloway 10 Sept 1791
William Brumley sec.
Brumley, Thomas C. m. Polly Hubbard 27 Dec 1821
Henry Tapscott sec.
Bryan, John m. Margaret L. Dameron dau. Thomas
Dameron 7 Jan ---- George D. Giddings sec
Bryant, Joseph m. Catherine Barrick 6 Sept 1841
Benjamin Armstrong sec.
Buchan, David m. Elizabeth H. Currell 9 May 1808
Thomas Pitman sec.
Buchan, David m. Nancy C. McTyre 7 Dec 1819, James
Brent sec.
Buchan, Nicholas P. m. Polly Beane 5 Feb 1816
Edward Beane sec.
Buchan, William m. Catherine Hinton 9 Oct 1779
John Fleet sec.
Burwell, Nathaniel m. Frances Wormeley 20 Apr 1786
Burroughs, John of Kempsville, Princess Anne County
Va. m. Elizabeth A. Snead 23 June 1846
Robert M. Johnston sec.
Burges, Charles m. Frances Fox, dau Ann Fox, 5 Oct
1721, David Ball sec.
Bush, Isaac m. Hannah Sammon 11 Oct 1720, Michael
Gill sec.
Bush, James m. Fanny Jarrett 8 Mar 1782, William
Rains sec.
Bush, James m. Frances Stott 13 Jan 1846, Thomas
D. Eubank sec.
Bush, Peter of Botetourt County m. Alice Rivier
29 Oct 1794, Peter Rivier sec.
Bush, Thomas m. Tomsey R. Thomas 11 Oct 1834
Thomas S. Dunaway sec.

Callahan, Thomas C. son of William Callahan m.
Elizabeth R. Blackmore 15 Apr 1828
William S. Ingram sec.
Callahan, Thomas C. m. Hannah F. Gresham 1 Apr
1842, William C. Gresham sec.
Callahan, William m. Nelly Chowning 30 Nov 1796
William Chowning sec.
Callahan, William C. m. Betsey Hunt 8 Oct 1817
William Callahan & John Hunt sec.
Camell, William of Northumberland County m. Sally
Kelley 14 Mar 1723, James Camell sec.
Cammell, George m. Elizabeth Stott 21 Sept 1737
Alexander Elliott sec.
Cammell, James m. Hannah Chilton 13 Aug. 1756
John Davis sec.

Cannaday, John of the Province of Maryland, m.
    Katherine Heale, dau. George Heale, dec.
    15 Jan 1736, Thomas Edwards sec.

Carney, James m. Polly Smith 19 June 1809, Vincent
    Carpenter sec.

Carpenter, Benjamin m. Hannah Wiggins (signed
    "Wiggon") 2 Apr. 1817, Thomas Jones sec.

Carpenter, Griffin m. Margaret C. Newgent 19 July
    1819, Thomas Newgent sec.

Carpenter, Heirome m. Lucy Pollard 29 Aug 1814
    Joseph Locke sec.

Carpenter, John m. Ellen Carter 18 Mar 1784
    William Carpenter sec.

Carpenter, Nathaniel m. Frances Blakesby 30 June
    1746, Thomas Edwards, Jr. sec.

Carpenter, Thomas m. Mary Michalls 13 Jan 1717
    Richard Flint sec.

Carpenter, William m. Sally Bailey 18 Aug 1794
    John Carpenter sec.

Carpenter, William C. m. Harriett Brown 21 Feb.
    John Briscoe sec.

Carpenter, William C. m. Molly Stonum 6 Aug 1818
    Robert D. Palmer sec.

Cary, John of Gloucester County m. Elizabeth
    Williams 23 Aug 1785

Carter, Addison L. m. Mary D. Jones 2 Jan. 1841
    William Jones sec.

Carter, Dale m. Dorothy L. Degges 15 Dec 1824
    John L. Degges, Jr. sec.

Carter, Edward m. Katherine Brent, Jr. 14 June
    1751, John Carter sec.

Carter, Edward m. Sally White 16 Feb 1786
    Joseph Carter sec.

Carter, Edward m. Judith Lunsford 21 May 1790
    Rodham Lunsford sec.

Carter, Edward m. Frances Kent 31 Jan 1822
    John C. Hinton sec.

Carter, George m. Elizabeth James 16 Nov 1780
    William James sec.

Carter, Henry m. Hannah Chilton 9 Aug 1758
    William Chilton sec.

Carter, Hiram m. Emily P. S. P. Tankersley 18
    Feb 18-- William Gibson sec.

Carter, Humphrey F. m. Frances Ravenscroft Ball
    dau. James Ball, 22 Nov 1815, William
    T. Yerby sec.

Carter, James m. (no name) 21 Sept 1807, Anthony
    Sydnor sec.

Carter, Job m. Sarah Rob, dau. Frances Rob, 11 Jan 1768, Joseph Carter sec.

Carter, Job m. Judith Harris 27 July 1778, George Miller sec.

Carter, Josiah m. Betty Dogget, dau. William Dogget 24 July 1753, John George sec.

Carter, Joseph m. Sarah Chilton 19 June, 1783, John Miller sec.

Carter, Joseph m. Margaret Carter 15 June 1792, Job Carter sec.

Carter, Joseph, Jr., widower m. Fanny Hutchings 1 June, 1797, Edward Newby sec.

Carter, Joseph A. m. Elizabeth C. Nutt 28 Oct 1817 Charles Taylor sec.

Carter, John m. Peggy Yerby 17 Mar 1785, John Carpenter sec.

Carter, John m. Martha Dillard 8 Nov 1786, William Chilton sec.

Carter, John m. Gracy B. Conway 19 Jan 1795, Spencer Carter sec.

Carter, John m. Carmin Pullen 24 Dec 1816, Thomas Carter sec.

Carter, John m. Mary Ann George Hammond 16 Apr 1821 Jesse Hammond sec.

Carter, Martin m. Milly Dunaway 16 Feb 1786 John Chowning sec.

Carter, Martin m. Salla Crain 17 Feb 1807, William B. Carter sec.

Carter, Ralph m. Sally B. Oldham 19 Apr 1830, John W. A. Edmonds sec.

Carter, Rawleigh m. Sarah Sharp 5 Sept 1765, Harry Carter sec.

Carter, Thomas m. Anne Hunton, wid. 15 Jan 1750 Thomas Edwards, Jr. sec.

Carter, Thomas m. Elizabeth Dogget 21 Nov 1771 William Griggs sec.

Carter, Thomas m. Judah Palmer 18 Nov 1799, Joseph Locke sec.

Carter, William m. Frances Brent 10 Nov 1747 George Wale sec.

Carter, William H. m. Harriott Ball 21 Feb 1832 Benjamin Waddey sec.

Carrell, Harry m. Amy Hains 23 July 1750, George Flower sec.

Carrell, Nicholas m. Margaret Lawson 18 July 1750 John Fleet sec.

Chichester, Richard m. Anne Fox, wid. William Fox, Gent. 11 July 1729, John Chichester sec.

Chichester, Richard m. Ellen Ball, dau. William
  Ball, 3 July 1734, Thomas Edwards sec.
Chichister, Richard m. Anne Gordon dau. James Gordon
  7 June 1759, Andrew Robertson sec.
Chitwood, William m. Betty Neal 18 May 1780, Robert
  Chinn sec.
Chitwood, William m. Nancy Thrift 20 Dec 1827, John
  Faucett & Griffin Jeffries sec.
Chitwood, William m. Mary Jane Barnes 9 Jan 1845
  Johnson Beane
Chilton, Andrew m. Elizabeth Davis 23 Dec 1788, John
  Hill, Jr. sec.
Chilton, Cyrus m. Leanna Beane 18 June 1804, Peter
  Beane sec.
Chilton, Edwin m. Betsey Chilton 24 Nov 1804, James
  Towles sec.
Chilton, Fauntleroy N. m. Sally G. Mitchell 24 Nov
  1824, Richard Mitchell sec.
Chilton, Griffin m. Elizabeth T. Kirk 29 Dec 1824
  Benjamin M. Walker sec.
Chilton, Henry m. Ann Flower 27 Dec 1783, John
  Flower sec.
Chilton, Hiram m. Polly Yopp 26 Nov 1818, Henry
  Tapscott sec.
Chilton, John R. m. Anna C. Chilton 8 Nov 1845
  A. Hill Currie sec.
Chilton, Jesse m. Ann Smith 19 Nov 1767, Moses
  Chilton sec.
Chilton, Jesse m. Nancy Gallaway 7 Nov 1796, John
  Hill sec.
Chilton, Jesse G m. Sally A. J. George, dau. Jesse
  George, 20 May 1844, Michael Wilder sec.
Chilton, Merryman m. Hannah Rogers 8 Feb 1805
  Thomas Myers sec.
Chilton, Norman m. Elizabeth Edmonds 22 Aug 1783
  Elias Edmonds sec.
Chilton, Richard m. Betsy Keeling 25 July 1827
  Thomas M. Owens sec.
Chilton, Robert N. m. Ann C. Chowning 19 Jan 1829
  John Chowning sec.
Chilton, Stephen m. Harriott Doggett 1 Apr 1817
  Chattin Dunaway sec.
Chilton, Thomas m. Winifred King 14 Jan 1723/4
  Jerome Pasquet sec.
Chilton, William m. Lucy Pitman 21 Oct 1822
  Elisman Pitman sec.
Chinn, Bartholomew m. Olivia Downman dau. J. B.
  Downman 8 June 1799, Henry L. Nutt sec.

Chinn, Bartholomew C. m. Million E. Downman 21 July
    Joseph W. Chinn sec.

Chinn, Christopher, son of Rawleigh Chinn, m.
    Agatha Thornton 26 Oct 1739, Thomas Thornton
    sec.

Chinn, Joseph m. Elizabeth Ball 2 May 1727, George
    Payne sec.

Chinn, Rawleigh, widower, m. Elizabeth Shearman 8
    Feb. 1797, Joseph Shearman sec.

Chinn, Thomas m. Sarah Mitchell 12 Nov 1735
    Thomas Edwards sec.

Chinn, Thomas m. Anne Edmonds 11 July 1752, Thomas
    Edwards, Jr. sec.

Chinn, Thomas, Jr. m. Sarah Brent 16 Oct 1764
    Thomas Edwards sec.

Chowning, Henry of Middlesex County m. Eunice Baily
    24 Aug 1769, John Baily sec.

Chowning, John S. m. Mary M. K. Mitchell 28 Nov
    1840, Daniel P. Mitchell sec.

Chowning, Leroy m. Cordelia C. Oldham 18 Nov 1839
    John Chowning sec.

Chowning, William m. Thomasin Sharpe 28 Dec 1764
    Hugh Brent sec.

Christian, Christopher m. Judah Davis 22 Oct 1761
    Benjamin George sec.

Christian, Christopher m. Easter Newsom 27 Dec 1788
    Peter Mason sec.

Christian, Francis m. Katharine Chinn, dau. Ann
    Chinn, 6 July 1756, Thomas Edwards, Jr. sec.

Christopher, George m. Amelia T. Parker 26 Oct 1839
    Thomas Christopher sec.

Christopher, John m. Dolly Fleet 19 July, 1781
    Henry Hinton sec.

Christopher, John F. m. Elizabeth Robinson 16 Dec
    1833, James Robinson sec.

Christopher, Thomas m. Achsah Dunaway 18 Mar 1808
    Rawleigh Dunaway sec.

Church, William m. Betsey Johnson Davis 17 Aug
    1801, Bartley Davis sec.

Church, William m. Ollin Gundry 12 Jan 1809, James
    L. Norris sec.

Churchill, William, of Middlesex County, m.
    Elizabeth Edwards 23 Sept 1762, Richards
    Edwards sec.

Clark, Benjamin D. m. Octavia A. Ball 17 Mar 1845
    John B. Ball sec.

Clark, Daniel m. Amey Shelton 15 May 1756, George
    Purcell sec.

Clark, John L. m. Elizabeth Oldham 4 June 1838
Turner Hanks sec.
Clark, Robert m. Judith Wilkinson 20 May 1786
William Warwick sec.
Clark, William m. Ann Clark 7 June 1843, Albert G.
Gibson sec.
Clarke, Gardner m. Judith Beane 3 Nov 1795, John
Beane sec.
Clarke, Humphrey m. Ann Kent 3 Oct 1838, Cyrus
Hazard sec.
Clarke, Jesse m. Elizabeth Miller 15 May 1786, Job
Carter sec.
Clarke, William T. m. Nancy Connely 7 July 1832
Addison Hall sec.
Clephon, Charles m. Judith Waugh, dau. Elizabeth
Waugh 27 June 1726, Alexander Campbell sec.
Coats, Rawleigh m. Catherine Dye 11 May 1786
Richard Dye sec.
Coats, Rawleigh m. Sarah Weblin 1 Jan 1780, Thomas
Riveer sec.
Coats, Thomas m. Sally Watts 18 Nov 1822, Thomas
Douglass sec.
Coats, Thomas m. Polly Seebry 29 July 1834, Griffin
Brown sec.
Coates, Richard m. Molly Garner 2 Nov 1813, Thomas
Warner sec.
Coates, Thomas m. Molly Coates 3 Aug 1816, William
Garner sec.
Cockarell, Presly of Northumberland County m.
Susanna Whaley, wid. 26 Mar. 1728, George
Evans, sec.
Cockarell, Richard m. Nancy Sampson 12 May 1812
Hiram Kain sec.
Coles, Richard P. m. Amanda Myers 19 June 1821
Rawleigh Dunaway sec.
Coleman, Richard m. Elizabeth Barrick, dau. Reubin
Barrick 29 Nov 1822, Benjamin M. Walker sec.
Coleman, Richard m. Mildred Palmer 17 June 1833
Thomas D. Davenport sec.
Conally, James m. Mary Smith 17 Dec 1825, William
Gresham sec.
Conally, William m. Margaret Hill 26 Dec 1792,
Jedithun James sec.
Conerly, William S. m. Judith C. Hazard 16 Dec 1833
Cyrus Hazard sec.
Conoly, William S. m. Noary L. Cockerill 16 Sept.
1844, William Davenport sec.

Connellee, Joseph m. Sophronia Ayres, dau. John
       Ayres 30 Nov 1843, James Connelle sec.
Connolly, John m. Mary Stephens 23 Apr 1778
       James Fendla sec.
Connolly, Patrick m. Ann Doggett 16 Apr 1772
       John Goodridge sec.
Connolly, Patrick m. ---- Connolly 27 Nov 1798
       William George sec.
Connolly, Williamson m. Nancy Rogers 18 Mar 1816
       John Rogers sec.
Coppeage, Cyrus m. Mary E. Hutchings 8 Apr 1843
       Joseph D. Pursley sec.
Cornelius, Bailey m. Milly Barnett 31 Dec 1831
       Benjamin G. George sec.
Cornelius, John m. Elizabeth Robins 16 May 1808
       Martin Shearman sec.
Cornelius, John m. Judith Hammonds 19 Nov 1838
       W. H. Stott sec.
Cornelius, James C. m. Sally James 5 May 1819
Cornelius, James C. m. Anna Walker 7 Jan 1841
       William Longworth sec.
Cornelius, Thomas m. Elizabeth Bottoms 22 Apr 1801
       Michael Wilder sec.
Cornelius, West m. Sarah Cornelius 11 May 1824
       John George sec.
Cornelius, William B. m. Mahalay Longworth 14 Feb
       Joseph G. Stephens
Cornelius, Thomas m. Elizabeth Dameron, dau. Aaron
       Dameron 26 May 1790, Aaron Dameron sec.
Corbin, George L. m. Sarah D. Spriggs 8 Dec 1817
       James Towles sec.
Corbin, Gawin m. Nancy Meredith 20 May 1811, James
       Pollard sec.
Cornish, George D. m. Jenny Percifull 2 Feb 1805
       -------- Thomas sec.
Costollo, John m. Sally Lunsford 28 Oct 1833
       Elias Fendla sec.
Cottrell, Thomas of Northumberland County m. Betsy
       Thomas 17 Jan 1799, Presley Cockarill sec.
Cottrell, William m. Judith Gibbs 22 Oct 1788, Luke
       Ashburn sec.
Covington, Thomas T. D. m. Ann Eliza Taylor 3 Feb
       1840, W. T. Dalby sec.
Cowles, William T. m. Sarah Sprigg 11 Apr 1838
       Thomas Sprigg sec.
Cowden, John m. Ann Garton 20 Aug 1804, Bartlett
       James sec.

Cox, Fleet m. Molly Webb 17 Jan 1814, John Yerby sec.

Cox, Fleet m. Elizabeth Kent 16 July 1821, Thomas Kent sec.

Cox, James m. Roxy Pinn 27 Oct 1842, Jesse Cox sec.

Cox, Jesse m. Elizabeth Tankersley 15 Oct 1845 George R. Waddey sec.

Cox, John m. Mary Wheeler 15 June 1789, George Phillips Oliver sec.

Cox, John m. Cretia Kemp 28 Dec 1819, Rawleigh Currell sec.

Cox, Presly of Westmoreland County m. Mary Fleet dau. Henry Fleet 17 Oct 1723, Henry Fleet sec.

Cox, Presley W. m. Martha A. Ingram 21 Feb 1827 Isaac Currell sec.

Cox, Presley m. Sarah Lock 2 Jan 1837, John L. Currell sec.

Cox, Thomas m. Jemima Kent, wid. 16 June 1790 William Cuthbert sec.

Craine, Isaac m. Sally Sullavant 24 Aug 1787 William Roebuck sec.

Creath, Jacob m. Milly V. Carter 24 Jan 1799, Job Carter sec.

Creswell, James m. Mary Garlington 9 June 1763 Fortunatus Sydnor sec.

Crittenden, Zachariah U. m. Mary F. Edmonds 21 Sept 1836, Benjamin Waddey sec.

Crow, Andrew m. Alice Pinckard 5 Sept 1809, Robert Angel sec.

Crowder, John m. Elizabeth S. Kent 3 Sept 1835 William C. Kent sec.

Crowder, Thomas m. Elizabeth H. Currell 20 May 1812 Isaac Hurst sec.

Crum, Joseph m. Cathan Thomas 16 Mar 1843, Mandred Vanlandingham sec.

Crump, Adam of Prince William County m. Ha---- Neale 6 Aug 1742, Thomas Edwards sec.

Crutcher, Richard m. Amanda Brown 6 Nov 1830 William Garrett sec.

Cullenden, George W. m. Susan C. Hall 7 Dec 1840 Addison Hall sec.

Cundiff, Benjamin m. Alcy McTire 13 Oct 1795 Charles Lee McTire sec.

Cundiff, Isaac m. Polly Basye 7 Dec 1825, Thomas M. Owens sec.

Cundiff, Isaac m. Pamala Carter 1 Dec 1828, Thomas P. Hill sec.

Cundiff, John m. Fanny Pinckard 20 July 1791, Henry Hudson sec.

Cundiff, John m. Ruth Nutt 20 Jan 1824, James Nutt sec.

Cundiff, Richard m. Ellen Forrester 2 Feb 1788 Edward Newby sec.

Cundiff, William m. Catherine Sullivant 19 Sept 1796, John Cundiff, Jr. sec.

Curd, John of Goochland County m. Lucy Brent 7 Apt 1758, William Stamp & Hugh Brent sec.

Curwell, James m. Jenetta Muse Conway 11 July 1787 Walker Conway sec.

Currell, Edward m. Elizabeth Sydnor 10 Apr 1790 John Chowning sec.

Currell, Fleet m. Sarah Currell Reaves 16 Nov 1790 Martin Shearman sec.

Currell, Fleet m. Mary James 6 Dec 1796, Charles James sec.

Currell, Isaac m. Dolly Hathaway 6 Jan 1782 Bartley James sec.

Currell, Isaac m. Polly S. Kent 17 July 1815 Thomas B. Oliver sec.

Currell, Isaac m. Mary L. George 6 May 1830 --------Gresham sec.

Currell, James, Jr. m. Frances James 20 May 1779 John James sec.

Currell, Jake m. Sally Currell 17 July 1815 Thomas B. Oliver sec.

Currell, John Y. m. Emily M. Mitchell 20 Dec 1848 Robert E. Beane sec.

Currell, Robert m. Mary King 20 Mar 1787, William Lawson sec.

Currell, Spencer m. Judith Bridgford 31 Dec 1757 Thomas Edwards, Jr. sec.

Currell, Spencer m. Lucy Hinton, dau. Catherine Buchan, 17 June 1793, John Christopher sec.

Currell, Thomas m. Mary George 17 Dec 1801, Henry C. Lawson sec.

Currell, William m. Lucy Kemm 14 July 1829, George D. Hayden sec.

Currell, William m. Elizabeth James 12 Jan 1836 John James sec.

Currell, William C. m. Frances M. George 24 Apr 1843, Daniel P. Mitchell sec.

Currill, Jacob m. Lucy Schofield 24 July 1790 Aaron Dameron sec.

Currill, Rawleigh m. Judith Cox dau. Thomas Cox 15 Apr 1794, Thomas Cox sec.

Currie, Armistead m. Jane M. Gilliam 12 Mar 1808 Ellyson Currie sec.

Currie, Armistead m. Mary Bathurst Jones Corbin dau
    Gawin Corbin sec
Currie, Armistead Hill m. Cordelia C. Chowning 13
    Mar 1847, George R. Waddey sec.
Curtis, Charles m. Ann George, dau. Spencer George
    21 Nov 1789, Spencer George sec.
Curtis, Hillary m. Betty Dogget 17 May 1771 Richard
    Hutchings sec.
Curtis, Nicholas m. Sarah Dameron, wid. 10 Oct 1797
    William Brown, Jr. sec.
Curtice, Thomas m. Betsey Chilton 12 May 1789, John
    Gordon, Jr. sec.
Cuthbert, William m. Ann Lawson, wid. 15 May 1790
    James Hill sec.

Damron, William m. Judith Gaskins 31 Jan 1834, John
    W. A. Edmonds sec.
Dameron, Dennis m. Elizabeth Haydon 9 Dec 1816
    Robert Persifull sec.
Dameron, George W. m. Ann H. Steel 20 Feb 1802
    Thomas Cornelius sec.
Dameron, Holland m. Betsey Williams 30 Apr 1800
    John Tapscott sec.
Dameron, John of Northumberland County m. Elizabeth
    Taylor 12 Sept 1728, Thomas Edwards sec.
Dameron, John m. Molly Brown dau. Elenor Brown 25
    Sept 1794, William Brown sec.
Dameron, Samuel m. Lucy Potts 17 July 1798, John
    Haydon sec.
Dameron, Thomas m. Sally Brown 26 Apr 1794, William
    Brown sec.
Dameron, Thomas m. Sally W. Roberts, dau. John
    Roberts 16 Jan 1799, Michael Wilder sec.
Daniel, Beverly m. Judith Brent Bailey 13 Mar 1803
    William Carpenter sec.
Daniel, Garrett m. Sally Riveer 8 Feb 1806, Martin
    George sec.
Daniel, Robert m. Hannah Rogers 22 Aug 1797, John
    Rogers sec.
Dance, Thomas m. Sally Hinton 4 June 1785, Samuel
    Hinton sec.
Danson, William m. Judith Jones Moore 20 June 1809
    Edward Currell sec.
Danson, William m. Frances A. Tarkleson 13 Oct
    1831, James G. Towles sec.
Dandridge, William H. m. Maria L. Jones 9 Mar 1825
    Thomas Hughlett sec.

Davenport, Daniel D. m. Sarah Hudnall 15 Dec 1806
     Fortunatus Davenport sec.

Davenport, Fortunatus of Richmond County m. Adaline
     Ann Latham 5 July 1837, James Latham sec.

Davenport, George m. Jane Harris 8 Mar 1784 William
     F. Dobyns sec.

Davenport, Joseph P. m. Lucy Simmonds 9 Dec 1817
     Thomas D. Davenport sec.

Davenport, Richard O. m. Lucy G. Hubbard 1 Jan 1838
     Jesse Hubbard sec.

Davenport, Willis W. m. Margaret C. Gresham 10 May
     1834, John Gresham sec.

Davis, Bartley m. Nancy Dodson 11 May 1799, George
     Dodson sec.

Davis, George m. Frances White 1 Jan 1779, John
     Goodridge sec. (badly damaged)

Davis, John, Jr. m. Caty McTyre 30 Dec 1766
     William King sec.

Davis, Jesse m. Elizabeth S. B. Barnet 9 Apr 1828
     Travis Seebry sec.

Davis, Joseph m. Susannah Church, dau. Samuel
     Church, 5 Feb 1791, Peter Beane sec.

Davis, Joseph m. Winifred Warwick 1 Dec 1794
     Benjamin Warwick sec.

Davis, Richard m. Mary Crowder 23 Jan 1787, John
     Crowder sec.

Davis, Capt. Richard m. Elizabeth Brown 5 Feb 1805
     Peter Beane sec.

Davis, Richard m. Sarah Chilton Dye 14 Feb 1815
     James Towles sec.

Davis, Robert m. Polly C. Percifull 16 Oct 1816
     Robert D. Palmer sec.

Davis, Thomas m. Patsey Fleming 2 Jan 1843, Leroy
     Beane sec.

Davis, William m. Mary Chilton (signed "Shealton")
     21 Mar 1839, Joseph Davis sec.

Dawson, David m. Ann Thomas 22 Mar 1842, William
     Beane sec.

Dawson, John m. Ann Thrall 7 Feb 1839, William C.
     Carpenter sec.

Dawson, William H. m. Maria Kirkham 19 Feb 1828
     William Kirkham sec.

Dawson, William m. Frances A. Tarkleson 13 Oct
     1831, James L. Towles sec.

Day, Robert m. Kitty Hill 22 Dec 1803, Henry C.
     Lawson sec.

Day, William m. Delia Lewin 17 Feb 1825, Armistead
Nickin & Shadrick Beo - - sec.

Deforrest, Cornelius m. Sarah Muse 1 Mar 1760
Martin Shearman, Jr. sec.

Degge, John m. Polly Brent 17 July 1809, Spencer
George sec.

Degge, William m. Mary Kirk 4 Sept 1788, Peter
Beane sec.

Degges, John m. Sary Hathaway 1 Dec 1801, Lawson
Hathaway sec.

Degges, William C. m. Amelia A. Degges 22 Oct 1835
John T. Degges sec.

Denny, John m. Roxy H. Lunsford 6 Dec 1836,William
O. Rains sec.

Dewbre, Robert m. Josephine T. Jesper 17 Jan 1842
William Saunders

Dickie, Adam of King & Queen County m. M. Ann
Thacker 7 May 1735, Charles Ewell sec.

Dies, Hiram J. m. Matilda P. Daugherty 17 May 1841
Thomas C. Callahan sec.

Digges, William of Gloucester County m. Catherine
King 21 July 1794, Lawson Hathaway sec.

Dillard, John m. Hannah McTyre dau. Robert McTyre
17 June 1761, Cornelius Deforrest sec.

Dines, Tyson m. Mary S. Stakes 30 Oct 1841
William Stakes sec.

Dix, Lewis H. m. Mary A. Tapscott, dau. Robert H.
Tapscott 16 Feb 1841, James E. Waddey sec.

Dix, Lewis H. m. Kitty Ann Brounley 10 Feb 1845
Benjamin Waddey sec.

Dobbs, Joseph m. Mary Schofield 22 Aug 1786, Jesse
Wilder sec.

Dobbins, Joseph G. m. Margaret Travis dau. Elizabeth
Travis 20 Dec 1841, Michael Wilder sec.

Dobyns, Edwin m. Catherine M Kirkmyre 8 Nov 1843
Bidkar George sec.

Dobyns, Christian L. m. Lucy Chowning 11 Dec 1809
James Chowning sec.

Dodson, Alexander m. Nancy Cotterall 25 Jan 1825
Lawson George sec.

Dodson, Richard m. Elizabeth G. George 13 Feb 1821
Zamoth George, Jr. sec.

Dodson, William m. Sabra Sullivant 30 June 1803
Joseph Sullivant sec.

Doggett, Benjamin m. Elizabeth Stott 19 Dec 1791
John Pullin sec.

Doggett, Benjamin m. Nancy P. Barrick 16 Oct 1820
Hugh B. Doggett sec.

Doggett, Coleman m. Mary Ann Hutchings 26 Oct 1798
John Hutchings sec.

Doggett, Dennis m. Nancy D. Webb 18 July 1803
Moses George sec.

Doggett, Elmore m. Mary Ann Hammonds 21 Jan 1779
Spencer George sec.

Doggett, Elmour m. Elizabeth Roberts 30 Mar 1786
William Doggett sec.

Doggett, Griffin m. Polly Hill 20 Dec 1810
William Connolly sec.

Doggett, George m. Judith Davis 19 Jan 1795 John
Hill sec.

Doggett, John, Jr. m. Judith Longwith 17 Aug 1795
John Longwith sec.

Doggett, John G. m. Siller Palmer 22 Mar 1808
Benjamin Doggett sec.

Doggett, James m. Betsey Doggett 17 Nov 1795
Peter Tankersly sec.

Doggett, James m. Sarah Doggett 15 Apr 1805 John
Doggett sec.

Doggett, Samuel m. Lucinda Wood Chilton 12 Dec
1815, Chatin Dunaway sec.

Doggett, Thomas m. Sarah Pitman 20 Dec 1830
Cyrus Hazard sec.

Doggett, William m. Mary Ann Doggett 3 Aug 1779
John Doggett sec.

Doggett, William m. Sarah George 16 June 1785
Moses George sec.

Doggett, William m. Judith Robb 15 Sept 1785
James Kelly sec.

Doggett, William, the younger, m. Catherine
Dunaway 18 Sept 1787, Robert Angell sec.

Doggett, William G. m. Nancy Cox dau. Thomas Cox
James Connally sec.

Doggett, William m. Charlotte Beane 20 Dec 1819
John Beane sec.

Doggett, William m. Catherine Pitman 14 Mar 1833
Thomas Pitman sec.

Dority, William m. Matilda P. Hill 13 Mar 1839
John H. Williams sec.

Douglas, Edward m. Elizabeth B. Bailey 29 July
1824, John Thrift sec.

Douglass, Richard m. Frances A. Reade 16 Dec 1841
Allen D. Reade sec.

Dove, James m. Nancy Flemming dau Charles Flemming
21 Feb 1772, William Graves sec.

Downing, Edward m. Hannah Ball 19 Sept 1796,George
    Ball sec.

Downing, Samuel m. Mary Robertson 22 Oct 1765
    Andrew Robertson sec.

Downing, Samuel, Jr. m. Catherine E. Payne 29 Mar
  1836 Benjamin Waddey sec.

Downman, Joseph m. Priscilla Downman dau. R. W.
    Downman, 14 Oct 1811, John B. Downman sec.

Downman, John B. m. Harriot Jane Downman 6 Jan
    1816, William Elmour sec.

Downman, Raleigh W m. Priscilla Chinn 25 May 1783
    Joseph B. Downman sec.

Downman, Rawleigh W. Downman m. Cordelia Gilmour
    28 Mar 1814, James Towles sec.

Downman, Rawleigh W. m. Elizabeth F. Curril 16
    Aug 1830, Robert T. Dunaway sec.

Downman, Travers of Northumberland County m. Anne
    Conway, wid. 28 Dec 1764, Thomas Edwards
    sec.

Downman, William m. Ellen Chichester, wid. 12
    June 1747, Thomas Edwards, Jr. sec.

Downman, William of Richmond County m. Susan
    Hudnall 18 Dec 1815, James Sheppard sec.

Dozier, Richard T. m. Nelly Norris 1 Jan 1808
    Rawleigh Norris sec.

Dozier, Thomas m. Huldy Hammond 26 Mar 1814 Henry
    & Hurst sec.

Dozier, Thomas m. Elizabeth D. Hazzard 4 May 1841
    Joseph Peirce sec.

Driver, William m. Alcy Hammond 9 June 1812 Lewis
    Hammond sec.

Dungan, David m. Nancy Branham Demerett, sister
    of Benjamin Demerett, 19 July 1793
    William Carpenter sec.

Dunton, Daniel m. Milly George 15 July 1799 Peter
    Beane sec.

Dunton, William m. Sarah George, dau. Benjamin &
    Catherine George, born 26 Feb. 1773 -
    8 April 1794, Nicholas L. George sec.

Dunton, William m. Juliett Hathaway 20 May 1820
    Thomas L. Lawson sec.

Dunton, William m. Elizabeth Hayden 2 Oct 1837
    George Kirkmyer sec.

Dunaway, Chattwin m. Milly Hill 14 Dec 1791
    Thomas Pitman sec.

Dunaway, Chattin m. Elizabeth Chilton 22 Aug 1815
    James Towles sec.

Dunaway, Epaphroditus m. Elizabeth T. Hathaway
dau. Lawson Hathaway 28 Apr 1842, Robert
T. Dunaway sec.

Dunaway, George C. m. Elizabeth Norris 16 Oct 1797
Edward Currell sec.

Dunaway, Henry m. Polly Talley 12 Dec 1835, George
Talley sec.

Dunaway, Henry m. Elizabeth Talley 1 Jan 1840
Joshua Beane sec.

Dunaway, Isaac m. Eliza Dunaway 9 Dec 1835, James
Tully sec.

Dunaway, James M. m. Ann C. Chilton 25 Dec 1843
Eppa N. Dunaway sec.

Dunaway, Joseph m. Nancy Wilder 21 Apr 1812, James
Tally

Dunaway, Joseph m. Nancy Angle 6 July 1816
Benjamin Doggett sec.

Dunaway, Opie m. Winny James Palmer 20 Sept 1802
James Towles sec.

Dunaway, Robert T. m. Frances Simmonds 14 Dec 1828
William H. Dandridge sec.

Dunaway, Robert T. m. Mary D. George 25 Sept 1837
B. M. Walker sec.

Dunaway, Rawleigh m. Frances E. Carter 27 Apr 1818
Eppa Norris sec.

Dunaway, Rawleigh m. Ann C. George dau. Lawson
George 18 Oct 1841, Robert T. Dunaway sec.

Dunnaway, Samuel m. Ann Davenport 18 Dec 1778
Ran: Davenport sec.

Dunaway, Samuel m. Sally Scurlock 14 Dec 1802
Samuel Scurlock sec.

Dunaway, Samuel m. Winneyford Umfrice 22 Jan 1831
Heiram Haynie sec.

Dunaway, Samuel m. Winneyford Winfried 22 Jan
1831, Heiram Haynie sec.

Dunaway, Thomas m. Jenny Riveer 6 Jan 1801 Thomas
Riveer sec.

Dunaway, Capt. Thomas L. m. Felicia T. Hall dau.
John Hall 19 Nov 1824

Dunaway, Urbam B. m. Frances McCartie 20 Jan 1834
R. T. Dunaway sec.

Dye, John m. Sally Day 16 Sept 1773 James Selden
sec.

Dye, John, Jr. m. Judith Chilton 5 Mar 1789
Richard Dye sec.

Eaton, Elijah m. Dorothy Davis 17 Aug 1787 John
    Roberts sec.
Edmonds, Elias B. m. Malana Jana Payne 13 Dec
    1838, Robert T. Dunaway sec.
Edmonds, John m. Jane W. Kent 20 Apr 1812 James
    Currell sec.
Edmonds, John m. Nancy Bland 5 April 1826
Edmonds, John W. A. m. Ann Y. Kirk 11 Dec 1828
    Robert Smith sec.
Edmonds, Ralph m. Grace Spiller 24 Mar 1809 Oliver
    Towles sec.
Edmonds, Ralph m. Frances B. Hall 1 Jan 1817
    Addison Hall sec.
Edmonds, Ralph m. Mary Ann Eustace 6 Mar 1827
    Benjamin Waddey sec.
Edmonds, Robert m. Anne Conway 10 June 1729
    Thomas Edwards sec.
Edmonds, Robert m. Elizabeth Lee Taylor 19 June
    1762, Isaac Taylor sec.
Edmonds, Robert m. Elizabeth L. George, dau.
    Zamoth George, 15 Jan 1838, Hiram P. James
    sec.
Edmonds, Thomas W. m. Ailcey O. Beale 2 Jan 1832
    George M. Downman sec.
Edwards, Charles m. Sarah Meredith dau. John
    Meredith 14 Sept 1775, Elias Edmonds sec.
Edwards, Charles, widower, m. Sally Lee 7 Mar 1797
    Henry C. Lawson sec.
Edwards, David m. Flowrinda F. Thatcher 28 July
    1825, Benjamin M. Walker sec.
Edwards, Edward m. Elizabeth L. Foddery 12 Dec 1806
    John Scbree sec.
Edwards, Elias m. Sophia Edwards 1 Mar 1832 Cyrus
    Riveer sec.
Edwards, Griffin m. Betsy Ledford dau. John Ledford
    2 June 1824, Opie Beane sec.
Edwards, Dr. John of Gloucester County m. Ann Swan
    13 July 1736, Thomas Cowards sec.
Edwards, John m. Margaret Towles 27 Oct 1814, John
    Nutt sec.
Edwards, Edward m. Ann Chinn 20 Feb 1750, Thomas
    Edwards sec.
Edwards, Thomas m. Sarah Swan 4 Aug 1722, William
    Payne sec.
Edwards, Thomas W. m. Ailcey O. Beale 3 Jan 1832
    George W. Dunaway sec.
Edwards, William m. Elizabeth Griggs dau Frances
    Wells 6 July 1730, Hugh Brent sec.

Edwards, William m. Franky Carter dau. Dale Carter
        18 Mar 1773, John Edwards sec.

Edwards, William m. Jeney Swanson 28 Jan 1807
        Epaphroditus Robinson sec.

Elgar, Samuel m. Hannah Steptoe dau. Joanna
        Hutchinson 16 Dec 1793, John Watts sec.

Elliott, Alexander m. Judith Davis 17 June 1794
        James Connally sec.

Elliott, Robert m. Sally Davis 7 Aug 1821, Moses
        Robinson sec.

Ellett, Thomas m. Sarah Lee 16 Sept 1779, Stephen
        Lock sec.

England, George m. Martha Conway Taylor 31 Dec 1814
        Robert Nutt sec.

England, George m. Matilda Westley Waddey 12 Jan
        1815, Richard Payne sec.

Eubank, Giles m. Caty Dunaway 18 Mar 1802 Eppey
        Norris sec.

Eubank, Warner m. Fanny Edmonds dau. Ralph Edmonds
        11 Jan 1842, Samuel Downing sec.

Eustace, Isaac m. Agatha Conway 15 Apr 1757, Thomas
        Gaskins sec.

Eustace, John m. Maria Leland 24 June 1808, Leroy
        P. Leland sec.

Eustace, John m. Margaret E. Payne 23 Aug 1833,
        Elias Edmonds sec.

Evans, Capt. Joseph m. Charlotte Garner, dau.
        Griffin Garner 11 Jan 1847, George W. Ford
        sec.

Evans, Robert m. Alcy T. Carter 3 May 1819, James
        Thrall sec.

Evans, Thomas m. Dorcas Carnelious 19 Feb 1787
        John Steptoe sec.

Everett, John D. m. Alice G. Harrison 1 Jan 1800
        James Towles sec.

Ewell, Charles m. Sarah Ball 22 Sept 1736, Thomas
        Edwards sec.

Ewell, James m. Mary Curle 18 Dec 1762, Stokely
        Towles sec.

Ewell, James m. Sarah Ann Conway 7 July 1783
        Edwin Conway sec.

Ewell, James m. Margaret Robertson 30 Nov 1794
        James Towles sec.

Ewell, James m. Mira Chowning 7 July 1836, B. M.
        Walker sec.

Ewell, Solomon m. Eve Taylor, wid. 10 Jan 1746/7
        John Edwards the elder sec.

Fallin, William m. Nancy Norris, Jr. 6 Jan 1805
    John Norris sec.

Fauntleroy, Griffin, Jr. m. Judith Heale 21 Oct
    1737, Thomas Edwards sec.

Fauntleroy, Moore, son of William Fauntleroy of
    Lunenburg in the County of Richmond m. Ann
    Heale 20 Dec 1736, Joseph Heale sec.

Fauntleroy, Robert m. Sarah Ball 2 Apr 1791
    Nathaniel Gordon sec.

Fendla, Elias m. Winna C. Haydon 24 Nov 1815
    William O. Haydon sec.

Fendla, Elias m. Hannah George 1 June 1835, Silas
    Beane sec.

Fendla, Elias m. Lucy Bottoms 5 May 1836, John K.
    Treakle sec.

Fendla, George m. Frances Carter 21 May 1762
    George Walker sec.

Fendla, John m. Sally Lee Schofield 15 Aug 1787
    Elias Schofield sec.

Fendlay, Thomas m. Nancy Jones 24 Feb 1789
    Anthony Kirk sec.

Fendly, James m. Janetta Carter 21 Dec 1819
    Thomas B. Oliver sec.

Ficklin, Joseph m. Easter Newby 3 Feb 1781
    Robert Chinn sec.

Filk, Amos m. Peggy Mason 25 July 1786, Peter
    Busk sec.

Fitzhugh, Henry of Stafford County m. Lucy Carter
    dau. Robert Carter, consent of Robert
    Carter dated 28 July 1730

Fitzhugh, Henry of Culpepper County m. Jane E.
    Downman 20 Nov 1837, John B. Branham sec.

Flemming, James m. Molly Ashbourn 2 Nov 1813
    William Flemming sec.

Flemming, William m. Sally Mason 31 Jan 1817
    George Webb sec.

Fleet, John m. Mary Edwards 29 May 1746, Thomas
    Edwards, Jr. sec.

Fleet, William m. Ann Jones 1 Nov 1718, George
    Wale sec.

Flippo, Joseph P. m. Eliza P. George dau.
    Benjamin George 1 May 1839, Warner Eubank
    sec.

Flippin, Armstead m. Elizabeth Schofield 28 Jan
    1834, John W. A. Edmonds sec.

Flint, Thomas m. Hannah Blackmore 11 Jan 1746/7
    John Rogers sec.

Flint, Thomas m. Silla Routt 18 Aug 1766, Richard
    Mitchell sec.
Flint, Thomas m. Priscilla Newby 30 Aug 1797
    Stokeley Towles sec.
Flower, George m. Susey Brent 21 Aug 1758, Francis
    Timberlake sec.
Flower, John m. Judith Mason 18 Apr 1803, James
    Towles sec.
Flowers, George, son of John Flowers, Sr. m.
    Elizabeth Robb 9 July 1800, William Meredith
    sec.
Flowers, John, Jr. m. Ann Nuttall 19 June 1797 John
    Flowers sec.
Flowers, John, Jr. Salley Carter 16 Mar 1801
    Spencer Carter sec.
Foote, Richard S. m. Mary L. McNamara 28 Dec 1831
    James Harding sec.
Ford, Daniel m. Elizabeth F. Currell, dau. Henry
    Currell 27 May 1773, Henry Towles sec.
Ford, Capt. George m. Mary Lawson, dau. Thomas
    Lawson 12 Aug 1777, Henry Lawson sec.
Ford, George m. Lucy Hill 11 Jan 1847, William
    Rowel sec.
Ford, James W m. Clarissa E. Taylor, dau.
    Thorowgood Taylor 12 Sept 1848, Hugh Brent
    sec.
Ford, John m. Mary Ann Jeff 28 Oct 1837, Michael
    W. George sec.
Ford, Thomas N. m. Frances H. George 7 Jan 1809
    William Pollard sec.
Forester, Thadeus m. Patsy P. Doggett 24 July 1838
    Joseph Tapscott sec.
Forrester, William of Richmond County m. Frances
    Bryant 13 July 1715, Thomas Bryant sec.
Forrester, William m. Ann S. Palmer 3 Mar 1831
    Edward Payne sec.
Foster, Joshua m. Sarah D. Allen 22 Feb 1821
    Richard Davis sec.
Frazier, John m. Mary Thomas wid. 14 June 1791
    John Doggett sec.
Francis, William m. Sally George 20 May 1817
    Joseph Shearman sec.
Frost, Alexander m. Sally George 12 Mar 1833
    William Owings sec.
Fullington, Alexander m. Lucy Walker 31 July 1807
    John Carpenter sec.

Gaines, James m. Nancy Waymouth 10 Mar 1824, Edward
    Payne sec.

Gallbreath, Robert of Middlesex County m. Margaret
    Carter, wid. ---- 18--, Thomas Edwards sec.

Galloway, James m. Nancy Knight 27 Dec 1786
    Samuel Sutton sec.

Galloway, James B. m. Ann F. Smither 9 Dec 1812

Galloway, Kemp m. Sukey Wallace 12 Apr 1799
    William Wallace sec.

Galloway, Kemp m. Sarah Snow 30 June 1808, John
    Waddey sec.

Galle, Severn m. Alcey F. Conway 7 Oct 1799
    Spencer Carter sec.

Ganes, John m. Polly Waymoth 3 Jan 1816, Nicholas
    P. Buckhard sec.

Garland, Griffin, widower, m. Frances Burwell, wid.
    16 Mar 1791, John Lehon sec.

Garlington, Christopher m. Elizabeth Conway, 5 May
    1724, Thomas Heath of Northumberland sec.

Garlington, William m. Lucy Currell, dau. George
    Currell, 8 Nov 1777, John Sydnor sec.

Garrett, William m. Margaret Brown 26 Mar 1830
    Thomas Bush sec.

Garner, Thomas m. Molly Coates 27 Feb 1811
    Rawleigh Coates sec.

Garner, Williamson m. Charlotte McTyre 24 Mar 1802
    William C. McTyre sec.

Garner, William m. Ellen Mercer 21 Nov 1782, Joseph
    Stephens sec.

Garner, William m. Kitty Shelton 27 Dec 1816
    Thomas Coates sec.

Garner, William m. Susan Brown 23 July 1823, John
    Beane, Jr. sec.

Garner, William m. Lucy Baily 20 July 1830, Edward
    Douglas sec.

Garner, William, Jr. m. Sarah Ann Bailey 16 Dec
    1839, Thomas C. Callahan sec.

Garner, William m. Sarah D. Barrick 17 June 1846
    Samuel D. Gresham sec.

Garten, Benjamin m. Mary Marsh 23 Feb 1842,
    Joseph Barrett sec.

Garton, Anthony m. Lettice Wheeler 20 Apr 1786
    Vincent Brent sec.

Garton, Benjamin m. Molly Reever 19 Jan 1788
    William Cornelious sec.

Garton, Samuel m. Polly Marling 19 Apr 1819
    William Gibson sec.

Gaskins, Edward W. m. Elizabeth H. Yerby 17 Feb
    1842, Thomas J. West sec.

Gaskins, Edward m. Eliza Swanson 1 Nov 1845, James
    R. Miller sec.

Gaskins, Joseph m. Sally Gaskins 1 Dec 1805, Edwin
    Gaskins sec.

George, Baily m. Nancy George 21 Mar 1797 Thomas
    James sec.

George, Benjamin m. Judith Doggett 31 Dec 1816
    Joseph L. Shearman sec.

George, Benjamin Griffin m. Catherine L. George,
    dau. Patsey George 19 Dec 1831, Nathan
    Spriggs sec.

George, Benjamin m. Dorinda Ingram 14 Feb 1837
    John W. Ingram sec.

George, Benjamin G. m. Susan P. Shearman 26 Feb 1837
    William H. Stott sec.

George, Capt. Bedkar m. Mary Degge 5 May 1812
    Oliver Towles sec.

George, Bidkar m. Matilda C. Dobyns 23 July 1830
    Robert N. Chilton sec.

George, Enoch m. Alice Martin Garland, dau. Frances
    Garland, 20 Sept 1808, O. Towles sec.

George, Enock m. Nancy Julia Myers dau. Thomas
    Myers 11 Dec 1816, William F. Yerby sec.

George, Fortunatus m. Judith Norris 20 Oct 1788
    Thomas Oliver sec.

George, Harrison C. m. Dorothy S. Carter 11 Nov
    1833, Silas Beane sec.

George, Isaac m. Winney Brown, dau. Spencer Brown
    11 Oct 1808, Oliver Towles sec.

George, James B. m. Mary M. Flint 3 May 1824
    Benjamin Waddy

George, James m. Ann Hammonds 1 Jan 1846, Lewis
    Hammonds sec.

George, Jeduthun m. Dorcas Tapscott 19 Oct 1780
    Edney Tapscott sec.

George, Jesse m. Judith Lunsford 9 Feb 1822, John
    Roberts sec.

George, John M. m. Ann C. Thrall 21 Dec 1830
    William Mason sec.

George, John m. Mary S. Currell 26 Sept 1837
    James C. Cornelius sec.

George, Lawson m. Judith Palmer 27 Sept 1816
    William F. Yerby sec.

George, Lawson m. Lucy Tapscott 24 Sept 1817
    James Brent sec.

George, Leonard m. Mariah R. Prosper 21 Dec 1835
    R. T. Dunaway sec.

George, Leroy N. m. Harriet J. Boatman, dau. Judith
    Boatman 5 Dec 1842, Abraham Wilson sec.

George, Martin m. Rebecca M. Stott 21 Jan 1823
    James Wilder sec.

George, Martin m. Jane M. Williams 19 Feb 1828
    William Mason sec.

George, Michael W. m. Judith N. George 15 Jan 1823
    John P. Shelton sec.

George, Michael W. m. Elizabeth Jefferson 24 Dec
    1827, James Wilder sec.

George, Michael W. m. Judith D. George 17 Aug 1836
    George W. Ford sec

George, Michael W. m. Ann S. Gains 5 Feb 1842 Peter
    Chase sec.

George, Monroe m. Ann Lunsford 17 Jan 1827 John B.
    Pullen sec.

George, Moses m. Alla Mason 20 May 1802, James
    Towles sec.

George, Moses m. Molly Chilton 3 July 1815, James
    Towles sec.

George, Newton, Jr. m. Ann Mealy 26 Dec 1834, John
    Mealy sec.

George, Nicholas m. Frances Connelly 10 June 1762
    William Tayloe sec.

George, Nicholas Lawson m. Susanna Tapscott 17 Apr
    1783, Elijah Percifull sec.

George, Octavius, son of Maria F. George m. Frances
    A. Towles, dau. Oliver & Kitturah Towles, 23
    Nov 1844, George H. Webb sec.

George, Spencer, Jr. m. Susanna Brent 21 Nov 1796
    George Brent sec.

George, Spencer m. Sarah E. Miller 15 Apr 1815
    James Towles sec.

George, Spencer m. Mary Pitman 9 July 1822, Daniel
    P. Mitchell sec.

George, Spencer m. Paulina Lawson dau. H. C. Lawson
    13 Nov 1826, George P. Stephens

George, Tarpley m. Elizabeth James 15 Feb 1790
    William Hutchings sec.

George, Tarpley m. Sarah Ann Wilder 2 June 1824
    William Jefferson sec.

George, Thomas N. m. Harriott Haydon 19 May 1823
    Thomas M. Owens

George, Thomas Dobyns m. Ann K. Patrick 11 Jan
    1827, William Payne sec.

George, Warren W. C m. Elizabeth Palmer dau. Sally
Palmer 29 Sept 1836, James W. Gresham sec.

George, Warren S. C., son of Jane George m. Louisa
A. C. Kidd 25 Jan 1837, Thomas Norris sec.

George, Wickliff m. Mary Towles 1 Jan 1822, Charles
Rogers sec.

George, William m. Molly Miner 2 Dec 1782, Martin
Norris sec.

George, William m. Elizabeth Linton Arms 2 July
1785, Samuel Moore sec.

George, William m. Barbara Dobyns 18 Aug 1794
Merryman Payne sec.

George, William, widower m. Sarah Wilder 9 Nov
1796, Gilbert Currell sec.

George, William m. Polly Chilton 2 Aug 1801
Bedkar George sec.

George, William m. Nancy Angel 31 Jan 1803
Bartley Overstreet sec.

George, William m. Behelhelam N. Payne 11 Apr
1806, Charles Simmond sec.

George, William m. Jane Hathaway 6 Jan 1816
John L. Chowning sec.

George, William m. Fanny Pullen 6 Mar 1817
Benjamin Waddey sec.

George, William H. m. Judith Sampson 11 Nov
1824, Martin Sampson sec.

George, William P. m. Lucy A. West 2 Mar 1837
Thomas J. West sec.

George, William P. m. Mary A. Palmer 9 May 1843
Joseph Barnett sec.

George, Zamoth m. Fanny Pearson 16 Mar 1786
William Meredith sec.

George, Zamoth m. Mary K. James 8 Apr 1805, John
James, Jr. sec.

George, Zamoth m. Nancy C. Currell 16 Dec 1818
Lawson Hathaway sec.

Gibson, John m. Molly Hunton 27 July 1803
William Gibson sec.

Gibson, Robert m. Ruth Wright, widow of Mottrom
Wright, 11 Dec 1701

Gibson, William m. Margaret L. Lawson 9 July 1822
Benjamin M Walker sec.

Gill, George m. Peggy Ball 25 June 1801 James
Towles sec.

Gilmour, John M. m. Cordelia Ball 30 June 1796
    Samuel Jessee sec.

Gilmour, Robert m. Sally McTyre 15 Feb 1810,
    Charles Wood sec.

Gilmour, William.m. Frances Downman 30 Sept 1823
    James W. P. Downman sec.

Gilbart, Ezekiel·of York County m. Winefred Gibson
    dau. Robert Gibson, 4 Sept 1722, Thomas
    Edwards sec.

Gilbart, Ezekiel m. Elizabeth Lawson 1 Aug 1749
    John Steptoe sec.

Glascock, George of Richmond County m. Judith
    Ball, dau. William Ball 13 Apr 1726
    William Ball sec.

Glascock, George of Richmond County m. Judith
    Mitchell 13 Jan 1748/9, Solomon Ewell sec.

Glascock, George m. Frances B. Berryman, dau.
    Sarah Berryman 24 Feb 1802, Samuel Oldham sec.

Glascock, Richard m. Ann S. Brent 5 Sept 1800
    James Towles sec.

Glascock, Richard M. of Richmond County m. Frances
    F. Edmonds, dau. Elias Edmonds 4 Apr 1808
    John Edmonds sec.

Glascock, Thomas m. Mary Ball 20 Jan 1759, Leroy
    Peachy sec.

Glascock, William of Richmond County m. Easter
    Ball, dau. Sarah Ball 10 Apr 1728, Thomas
    Edwards sec.

Glascock, William, Jr. m. Elizabeth Chichester 20
    Jan 1752, William Glascock sec.

Goodridge, Richard m. Anna Riveer 19 Nov 1764
    Joseph Norris sec.

Goodridge, William of Orange County m. Catherine
    Martin Hinton 17 Dec 1793, Henry Hinton sec.

Goodridge, William m. Ann Flint 16 Nov 1795
    Thomas Flint sec.

Good, Edmond m. Mary Chilton 28 Mar 1823, Hierom
    Carpenter sec.

Good, James m. Frances Shelton 28 Aug 1818, Elias
    Fendla sec.

Gordon, James, Jr. m. Elizabeth Gordon, sister of
    James Gordon 13 Aug 1777, James Tapscott sec.

Gordon, James m. Nancy Mitchell, dau. Thads,
    Mitchell 17 Dec 1832, Joseph R. Mitchell sec.

Gordon, John m. Betty Lee Ball, granddaughter of
    Joseph Ball 31 Oct 1787, Henry Towles sec.

Gordon, Joseph m. Mary Ann Brown 2 Oct 1844, John
  Brown sec.
Graham, Reginald m. Mary Ball, wid. 3 Apr 1774 John
  Taylor sec.
Gresham, George m. Mary James 25 Apr 1798, Bartley
  James sec.
Gresham, James W. m. Ann E. R. Armstrong 17 Oct
  Octavius Lawson sec.
Gresham, John m. Margaret Chowning 19 Oct 1807
  William Chowning sec.
Gresham, John m. Margaret M. Hughlett 21 Sept 1847
  Benjamin P. Warwick sec.
Gresham, Samuel m. Sarah G. Chilton 16 May 1831
  Richard Mitchell sec.
Griffin, Leroy m. Judith Ball dau. Joseph Ball
  3 Nov ,772, John McKay sec.
Griffin, LeRoy of Richmond County m. Mary Ann
  Bertrand 5 Oct 1734, Thomas Edwards sec.
Griffin, LeRoy of Richmond County m. Alice Currie
  dau. David Currie 28 July 1764, William
  Griffin sec.
Griggs, Thomas m. Judith Kirk dau. Sarah Kirk
  6 May 1768, George Phillips sec.
Griggs, Thomas m. Alcey Carter dau. Thomas Carter
  1 Oct 1772, William Brent sec.
Griggs, William m. Ruth Everitt 17 Nov 1777, John
  Selden sec.
Gundry, John m. Elizabeth Ellett 14 Apr 1796
  George Thatcher sec.
Gundry, John m. Judith H. Talley 18 Feb 1817
  George Talley sec.
Gundry, John M. m. Harriet J. George 13 May 1844
  Benjamin Waddey sec.

Hack, Nich° of Northumberland m. Elizabeth Howson
  dau. Sarah Ball, 16 May 1717, Richard Neale
  sec.
Hack, Tunstall of the Province of Maryland m.
  Hannah Conway 22 Apr 1746, Thomas Edwards,
  Jr. sec.
Hackny, Richard m. Filicia Kesterson 8 Dec 1834
  Joseph R. Mitchell sec.
Hall, Addison m. Susan Edmonds 1 Jan 1817, Ralph
  Edmonds sec.
Hall, John m. Mary T.K. Gibson 13 Sept 1825
  James Kirk sec.
Hale, Francis T. of Fauquir County m.Olivia Ball
  dau. Mary Ball 16 Dec 1824, D. Fauntleroy
  sec.

Hamilton, John m. Louisa D. Hill 28 Mar 1839
    Thomas Ingram sec.
Hammond, Charles m. Ann Gibbons Carter 9 Aug 1793
    John Carter sec.
Hammond, George C. m. Lucy B. Haydon 11 Mar 1845
    James Hammond sec.
Hammond, James m. Elizabeth Dameron 7 June 1814
    Jesse Hammond
Hammond, James m. Sarah A&E. Edwards 5 Aug 1840
    Joseph T. Haydon sec.
Hammond, Jesse m. Nancy Chilton 10 June 1802
    John Henry sec.
Hammond, Lewis m. Lucy Hammond 16 Oct 1820,John
    Lowry sec.
Hammond, Thomas m. Mary Lewis Tapscott 6 Nov 1792
    James Tapscott sec.
Hammonds, James m. Catherine Tapscott 17 June
    1784, John Tapscott sec.
Hammonds, James m. Winifred Boyd 21 Nov 1796
    William Gibson sec.
Hammonds, John m. Jean Chowning 30 Nov 1789
    Lewis Lunsford sec.
Hammonds, John, widower m. Mary Hazard,wid. 29
    Feb 1792, John Hewy sec.
Hammonds, William m. Catherine Dunton,dau. Sarah
    Dunton 6 July 1818, William Dunton sec.
Hanks, John m. Elizabeth Newgent 19 Nov 1816
    Thomas Newgent sec.
Harrison, Richard m. Ann Reade 18 May 1717
    Thomas Purcell sec.
Harman, Daniel H. m. Sarah George 22 May 1805
    Rawleigh Tapscott sec.
Harding, Cyrus of Northumberland County m. Mary
    Goodridge, dau. Richard Goodridge, 13 Sept
    1791, William Goodridge sec.
Harding, James m. Frances E. McNamara 26 Aug
    1826, Job Slocum sec.
Harding, John H. m. Frances Josephine Lemoine
    dau. F. Lemoine, Sr. 27 Dec 1827, Fereal
    Lemoine, Jr. sec.
Harding, William H. m. Ann H. George 6 Sept,
    1841, Robert T. Dunaway sec.
Harvey, Mungo m. Priscilla Ball 18 Aug 1769
    George Heale sec.
Harvey, Onesepharus m. Rebecca M. George 15
    May 1815, William T. Yerby sec.
Harvey, Onesephrun m. Felicia Towles 6 Mar 1822
    Benjamin M. Walker sec.

Harcum, William Wildy m. Patty Williams 21 July 1774
George Rust sec.

Harcum, William P. m. Frances H. Towell dau. Mark
Towell, 15 Sept 1826, John Meredith sec.

Harcum, Samuel m. Polly Gresham 21 Jan 1821 Daniel
P. Mitchell sec.

Hathaway, Henry m. Harriet E. Edmonds 16 Nov 1846
Ralph Edmonds sec.

Hathaway, John m. Jenny P. Newby, dau. Elizabeth
Newby, 28 Dec 1801, Charles Bailly sec.

Hathaway, Lawson m. Agnes Locke 11 Mar 1820, Addison
Hall sec.

Hathaway, Thomas m. Elizabeth Kirk 18 Nov 1772
William Lawson sec.

Hathaway, Thomas m. Jincy Chowning ---- 1804,
Portens Towles sec.

Hathaway, William m. Molly Currell 15 Aug 1798, John
Hathaway sec.

Hawkins, John m. Sarah Cornelious 18 June 1795,
Hugh Brent sec.

Haynie, Bridgar m. Sarah Shearman 16 June 1766
Martin Shearman sec.

Haynie, Cyrus m. Judith Lunsford 17 Dec 1816
William Lunsford sec.

Haynie, Daniel, of Northumberland County m. Judith
Fleet 9 Sept 1779, George Glascock, Jr. of
Richmond County sec.

Haynie, Garrett m. Amanda M. F. Norris 20 Dec 1847
William O. Norris sec.

Haynie, John m. Ann Conway Tapscott 7 Nov 1774
John Clayton & John Tapscott sec.

Haynie, Samuel m. Ann Carter 15 Mar 1781, Rodham
Lawson sec.

Haynie, Warner m. Lucy P. Carpenter 2 Jan 1837
Hancock Haynie sec.

Haynie, William of Northumberland County m. Ann
Edwards, wid. 16 Oct 1747, Thomas Edwards sec.

Hayden, Ezekiel m. Lucy Doggett, dau. William
Doggett 30 May 1788, Thomas Hayden sec.

Hayden, Ezekiel m. Elizabeth W. Cox 27 June 1828
William Kirkmeyer sec.

Haydon, Armistead m. Nancy P. Haydon 3 Apr 1810
Thomas Haydon sec.

Haydon, Charles m. Nancy Myres, wid. 2 Jan 1793
Thomas Revere sec.

Haydon, Hiram m. Mary Treakle 15 Aug 1836, Samuel
Treakle sec.

Haydon, Hiram m. Alice Ashbourn dau. Griffin
Ashbourn 12 Jan 1843, William M. Gatewood sec.

Haydon, John m. Elizabeth Potts 29 Dec 1788 Ezekiel
Haydon sec.

Haydon, Joseph m. Lucy B. Hammond, dau. Elizabeth
Hammond 9 May 1835, Michael Wilder sec.

Haydon, Lewis m. Alice Hurst, dau. Jane Hurst 15
Apr 1811, John Haydon sec.

Haydon, Thomas m. Polly Sampson dau. Nancy Sampson
6 Apr 1805, Thomas Oliver sec.

Haydon, Warner m. Dolly Barnett 4 Feb 1833, William
C. Callahan sec.

Haydon, Willis m. Elizabeth Carter, dau. Spencer
Carter 28 Jan 1801, Thomas Kent sec.

Haydon, William m. Peggy Sullivant, dau. Judith
Sullivant 14 Mar 1792, Ezekiel Haydon sec.

Haydon, William m. Mary Ann Doggett 20 Jan 1794
Ezekiel Haydon sec.

Hays, Thomas J. m. Elizabeth Mitchell 15 June 1812
John Hull sec.

Hazard, Alexander m. Judith Davenport 19 Dec 1796
Charles L. McTire sec.

Hazzard, Cyrus m. Polly Hill 22 Dec 1824, James
Brent sec.

Hazard, Cyrus m. Mary A. Spilman 19 Apr 1845
Warner C. Lunsford sec.

Hazard, Elias m. Mary Rogers 10 Dec 1792, John
Carpenter sec.

Hazard, Henry m. Harriet Alfred 7 Sept 1841, James
Bush sec.

Hazard, Joseph m. Mary Elizabeth Ashbourn 23 Mar
1841, Edward Payne sec.

Hazard, William m. Elizabeth D. McTyre dau.
Elizabeth Pinckard 22 Dec 1827, Kendall
McTyre sec.

Hazzard, William m. Frances Bryant 21 Jan 1836
Thomas English sec.

Headley, William W. m. Juliet Riveer 4 Aug 1842
L. S. Winstead sec.

Heale, George m. Sarah Smith 20 Jan 1746/7
Baldwin M. Smith sec.

Heale, William m. Judith Swan 22 July 1734, Thomas
Edwards sec.

Hendley, John m. Hannah Doggett 12 Apr 1797
Charles Webb sec.

Hening, John A. m. Mary E. L. Brent 6 Oct 1829
James E. Lawson sec.

Hill, Eppa m. Polly Chowning Carter 13 Feb 1817
Griffin Doggett sec.

Hill, James m. Betty Stephens 25 Dec 1781 Johathan
James sec.

Hill, James m. Nancy Connally 21 Dec 1786,
Jedithon Jones sec.

Hill, James M. m. Catherine E. Dix 18 Sept 1839
Lewis H. Dix & John Gresham sec.

Hill, John of Northumberland m. Elizabeth Martin
9 Jan 1735, Nicholas Martin sec.

Hill, John m. Alice Pitman 19 Sept 1814, Elias
Fendla sec.

Hill, John m. Hannah Yopp 31 Aug 1825, Benjamin
M. Walker sec.

Hill, Thomas m. Alice Spilman 21 Dec 1829 Charles
Ingram sec.

Hill, William m. Mary Merryman 24 Dec 1803 Thomas
Merryman sec.

Hill, William m. Winney Chilton Moore 2 Jan 1815
John Hill sec.

Hilton, William m. Ann Warwick 15 June 1815, John
Kemm sec.

Hinton, Archibald m. Nancy Kent 15 Nov 1813
Samuel M. Shearman sec.

Hinton, Fleet m. Catherine Pope 17 Nov 1768, John
Pope sec.

Hinton, George m. Catherine Kent 13 Nov 1834
James S. Towles sec.

Hinton, Henry m. Anna Fleet 23 June 1766, Thomas
Hinton sec.

Hinton, James M. m. Thomas Schofield 12 Dec 1842
Thomas Schofield sec.

Hinton, John m. Molly Brooks 21 Dec 1798, James
Towles sec.

Hinton, Richard m. Mary Ingram 17 July 1798, Henry
Hinton sec.

Hinton, William m. Judith Hill 24 Mar 1824
Richard Ingram sec.

Hipkins, Robert m. Ann Ball 22 Jan 1800, Stokely
Towles sec.

Hobson, William of Northumberland County m.
Judith Fleet 28 June 1723, Thomas Edwards &
Henry Fleet sec.

Holliday, Needham m. Amanda M. Robertson 6 Dec
1828, Alfred J. Rains

Holmes, John m. Polly E. Buchan dau. Nicholas P.
Buchan 12 May 1845, Stokeley H. Robertson
sec.

Howson, Leonard of Northumberland County m. Anne
    Fleet 10 Nov 1722, Henry Fleet sec.
Hubbard, Elias m. Judith George 14 Sept 1786
    Benjamin George, Jr. sec.
Hubbard, Ephriam m. ----nnah Edmonds 15 July
    1749, William Sanders sec.
Hubbard, Jabez m. Elizabeth Kirk 6 Jan 1808 John
    W. Revere sec.
Hubbard, Jesse m. Polly B. James 5 Jan 1814
    William T. Yerby sec.
Hubbard, Joseph m. Rebecca George 21 Sept 1780
    Elias Edmonds sec.
Hubbard, Thomas m. Ann Yopp 2 Jan 1783, Charles
    Hubbard sec.
Hubbard, William m. Elizabeth Boatman 17 May
    1756, Edward Ker sec.
Hubbard, William m. Judith Yopp 3 Jan 1785 James
    Carter & John Doggett sec.
Hudson, George m. Elizabeth West 12 Dec 1779
    James Waddy sec.
Hudson, Henry m. Amice Pitman 17 Mar 1786 Andrew
    Chilton sec.
Hudnall, Alfred m. Jane O. Beane 21 Nov 1836
    James Hurst sec.
Hughs, Thomas m. Judith Hill 16 Sept 1799 Joshua
    Crowder sec.
Hughlett, Augustine m. Sarah George 28 July 1806
    Ephraim Hughlett sec.
Hughlett, Bede m. Hannah H. Oliver 7 Jan 1813
    George B. Oliver sec.
Hughlett, Bede m. Polly Haydon 8 May 1833
    William George sec.
Hughlett, Ephraim m. Barbara Spilman 21 May 1801
    Renney Palmer sec.
Hughlett, Ephraim m. Molly George 28 Dec 1806
    Daniel Dunton sec.
Hughlett, John m. Roxillana Spiller 10 Dec 1708
    Benjamin Spiller sec.
Hughlett, Martin m. Latice Presley dau. Charles &
    Hannah Presley, born 12 Dec 1784, 13 Dec
    1809, Ephraim Hughlett sec.
Hughlett, Martin m. Lucy Webb 2 Dec 1813,William
    Pollard sec.
Hughlett, Robert m. Caroline S. Kirk, dau.
    Elizabeth B. Kirk 4 Jan 1848 Benjamin P.
    Warwick sec.
Hughlett, Roston m. Nancy Short 31 Dec 1811
    Ephraim Sprigs sec.

Hughlett, Royston m. Lucy Pollard, dau. Mary Hill
19 Mar 1818, E. Hill sec.
Hughlett, William E. m. Margaret H. M. Mitchell
29 June 1829, Rawleigh D. Carter sec.
Hughlett, Yarrat m. Sally Berryman dau. Sarah
Berryman 3 Sept 1788, Thomas W. Hughlett sec.
Hull, m. Sally Ball 19 Feb 1822, David Ball sec.
Hunt, John m. Elizabeth Lawson 22 Dec 1774, Robert
McCleoy sec.
Hunt, John m. Ellen Blade 16 Mar 1779, Henry
Currell sec.
Hunt, John m. Lucinda Brent 20 June 1796, Vincent
Brent sec.
Hunton, John m. Hannah Cortes 18 Nov 1779, George
Glascock sec.
Hunton, John W. m. Mary Pollard dau. James Pollard
15 May 1794, James Pollard sec.
Hunton, John W. m. Mary Hutchinson 28 July 1819
William O. Haydon sec.
Hunton, John W. m. Ann Doggett 30 Apr 1821, John
Edwards sec.
Hunton, John W. m. Nancy Dunaway 24 Oct 1827
Samuel B. Angel sec.
Hunton, Thomas m. Mary Currell 13 Nov 1722, Robert
Horton sec.
Hunton, Thomas m. Ann Wale 15 Nov 1734, Thomas
Edwards sec.
Hunton, Thomas m. Elizabeth Hinton, wid. 30 Dec
1774, James Newby sec.
Hunton, Thomas m. Betty Yerby 20 May 1779, William
Gibson sec.
Hunton, Thomas m. Ann Pope 16 Mar 1789, John
Goodridge sec.
Hurst, Isaac m. Nancy Lawson 17 Mar 1805, William
Smither sec.
Hurst, James m. Athaliah A. Jones 21 Nov 1843
Samuel Gresham sec.
Hurst, John m. Cordelia Norris 21 Jan 1823
Richard Nicken sec.
Hurst, Warner m. Susan Spiller 15 Oct 1801, Martin
Shearman sec.
Hutchings, Hugh m. Nancy Biscoe 23 Dec 1822
Robert Biscoe sec.
Hutchings, John m. Sally Miller 21 Jan 1778, John
Miller sec.
Hutchings, John m. Elizabeth Tankersly 17 Mar
1794, Peter Tankersly sec.

Hutchings, John m. Polly Biscoe 16 Nov 1818, Robert
     Biscoe sec.

Hutchings, Richard m. Milly Beane, dau. John Beane
     17 Dec 1791, Peter Beane sec.

Hutchings, Richard m. Molly Blakemore 16 Aug 1813
     William Blakemore sec.

Hutchings, Richard m. Elizabeth Hathaway 16 Dec 1822
     John Hutchings sec.

Hutchings, Thomas m. Louisa A. Yerby 14 Oct 1835
     Richard Hutchings sec.

Hutchinson, Hill W. m. Molly Pearson 8 Jan 1805
     James Towles sec.

Ingram, Charles m. Elizabeth Garton, dau. Rachel
     Crowder, 15 Apr 1799, Henry Hinton sec.

Ingram, Charles m. Margaret Ann Beane 1 Jan 1840
     ------Beane sec.

Ingram, Charles m. Mary C. Biscoe 22 July 1841
     William H. Kirk sec.

Ingram, George m. Martha Ann Johnson, dau. Ralph
     Johnson 19 Dec 1825, Thomas L. Lawson sec.

Ingram, Griffin m. Mary A. D. Flowers 22 Jan 1835
     John W. Flowers sec.

Ingram, Griffin m. Frances H. Selba 31 Jan 1837
     Daniel P. Mitchell sec.

Ingram, James m. Leah Hinton 16 June 1825, John C.
     Hinton sec.

Ingram, James m. Sally L. Flippin 30 Dec 1836
     James Gains sec.

Ingram, John F. m. Susanna Hinton, dau. Ann
     Hinton 13 Dec 1802, Lawson Hathaway sec.

Ingram, John m. Ann N. Brent 12 Aug 1811, Hugh
     Brent sec.

Ingram, Samuel M. m. Ann B. Robertson 6 May 1837
     Thomas S. Ingram sec.

Ingram, Thomas m. Sarah Fleet 16 Apr 1772, Spencer
     Hinton sec.

Ingram, Thomas m. Sarah Hinton 29 June 1827
     Ezekiel Hayden sec.

Ingram, Thomas S m. Rebecca M. James 1 Jan 1835
     James Fiendlay sec.

Ingram, William S. m. Tomsey S. Callahan 6 Nov 1826
     William Callahan sec.

Ingram, William S. m. Elizabeth Lattimore 24 Nov
     1829, Thomas L. Lawson sec.

Ingram, William m. Mary E. Kellum 13 May 1834
     Henry L. Briscoe sec.

Isles, Absalom m. Betsey Webb 15 Apr 1794, Peter
Mason sec.

Jackson, Benjamin m. Sally Jones 17 June 1805, John
Nicken sec.

James, Bartley m. Elizabeth Hathaway 20 Dec 1763
John Hathaway sec.

James, Bartley m. Elizabeth Waugh 17 Jan 1771

James, Bartley m. Amy Yopp 16 Feb 1795, Vincent
Brent sec.

James, Bartlet m. Susanna Ingram 23 June 1812
Oliver Towles sec.

James, Bartley m. Salley N. Brent 19 May 1817
Thomas James sec.

James, Charles m. Sally Hubbard 7 Jan 1804, G.
Smither sec.

James, David H. m. Elizabeth H. Carter 28 Nov
1826, John Longworth sec.

James, Hiram P. m. ----Dinns, dau. Ruth Dinns 5
Aug 1824, John N. Hunt sec.

James, James B. m. Elizabeth C. Lawson dau. Judith
N. Lawson 28 Nov 1843, Hugh Brent sec.

James, John m. Betsy L. Hinton 29 Apr 1811
William Pollard sec.

James, John m. Ann Pitman 8 Jan. 1834, Isaac
Pitman sec.

James, Matthias m. Judith Hinton 20 Jan 1790
William Hinton sec.

James, Robert m. Charlotte Locke, dau. Joseph
Locke 12 Nov 1805, John W. Revere sec.

James, Richard m. Elizabeth Currell 17 Apr 1822
William Gibson sec.

James, Thomas m. Elizabeth Brent, wid. 7 Sept
1795, Vincent Brent sec.

James, Thomas m. Judith Marsh 12 Nov 1826, John
Fawcett sec.

James, Thomas m. Polly B. James 15 Apr 1829
Vallentine H. Vowell sec.

James, Thomas m. Rebecca M. George 5 Mar 1831
Robert S. Brent sec.

James, William m. Nancy Ellett 13 Apr 1780
William Biscoe sec.

James, William M. m. Catherine M. Carter, dau.
Martin Carter 6 Apr 1808, Thomas Mason sec.

James, William M. Jr. m. Margaret Ann Hinton
1 Jan 1844, Cyrus Hazard sec.

Jeffries, Griffin m. Elizabeth Payne 30 Mar 1825
Thomas Douglass sec.

Jeffries, William m. Lucy Sebree 17 Sept 1798,
        John Morrison sec.
Jefferson, David m. Elizabeth Mason 8 Oct 1832
        John K. Treakle sec.
Jesse, Samuel m. Catherine George, dau. Frances
        George 2 Dec 1793, Richard Tapscott sec.
Johnson, George m. Elizabeth Blackmore 1 Feb 1786
        William George sec.
Johnson, Henry m. Ann Weaver 13 Feb. 1795,Richard
        Nicken sec.
Johnson, William m. Morning Bond 24 July 1804
        Andrew Chilton sec.
Jones, David m. Rhoda Jones 8 Aug 1795, James
        Jones sec.
Jones, Daniel m. Rachel Howe dau. Peter Howe 12
        June 1794, James Connally sec.
Jones, Francis, of Warwick County m. Jane
        Armistead 18 Dec 1770
Jones, Henry m. Margaret Lewin 30 Oct 1839, John
        Jordan sec.
Jones, James m. Winifred Boling 26 Nov 1795
        Daniel Jones sec.
Jones, John of Middlesex County m. Sarah Ball,
        dau. Margaret Ball 30 Sept 1747, William
        Montague sec.
Jones, John of Orange County m. Mary Bell 2 Nov
        1750, Thomas Heydon, Jr. sec.
Jones, John m. Betsy Weaver 17 Apr 1826, James
        Brent sec.
Jones, John m. Betsey Bell 19 Dec 1831,Armistead
        Nicken sec.
Jones, Lewis m. Milley Chilton dau. William
        Chilton sec.
Jones, Thomas m. Judith Sorrel 1 Jan 1802,James
        Towles sec.
Jones, William m. Frances Gilmour 30 June 1830
        William T. Jesse Sec.
Jones, William of Northumberland County m. Ann
        Bell, dau. John Bell 12 Mar 1740, John
        Bell sec.
Jones,Williamson C. m. Athaliah Ann Mitchell 8
        Nov. Richard Mitchell sec.
Jordan, John m. Harriet L. Lewis 23 Jan 1833
        Armistead Nickin & Cyrus Nickin sec.
June, Travis D. m. Jane Stott 20 Dec 1825,John
        C. Warwick & John Fawcett sec.

Keene, Newton m. Sarah Edwards 14 Apr 1749,Thomas
       Edwards sec.
Keene, William of Northumberland County m.
       Elizabeth Ball, 2 Nov 1721, Thomas Edwards
       sec.
Kelly, John m. Sarah Norris 5 Jan 1792, John Lehon
       sec.
Kelly, James m. Judith Cammell 16 July 1778, John
       James sec.
Kelly, William m. Elizabeth Riley, wid. 6 Apr 1745
       John Wale sec.
Kelley, John m. Sally Veaney 12 May 1847, Leroy
       Lewin sec.
Kelley, James m. Hannah H. Tapscott 25 Jan 1799
       William George sec.
Kelley, James m. Amy Y. Hubbard 21 Nov 1842, Jesse
       Hubbard sec.
Kem, John m. Elizabeth Davis 9 Oct 1833, James
       Seebry sec.
Kem, John E. m. Mariah H. Ball 7 Apr 1847,Hilkiah
       Ball sec.
Kemm, John m. Mary Hazard 20 Oct 1823, John Rogers
       sec.
Kemm, Richard m. Sally B. Brown 16 Dec 1801, John
       Carpenter sec.
Kemm, Richard R. m. Winifred Thomas 24 Dec 1828
       William T. Kemm sec.
Kemp, John m. Chrissy Cox 8 Sept 1801, Edward
       Currell sec.
Kemp, John m. Jennette Chilton 24 Sept 1829
       Michael W. George sec.
Kenner, William m. Betty Myars 11 Oct 1774
       Thomas Smith sec.
Kenner, Waring m. Mary Ingram, dau. Thomas Ingram
       30 Dec 1844, Thomas Schofield sec.
Kent, Beverly m. Ann C. Danson 17 Dec 1838
       William E. Waters sec.
Kent, Daniel m. Mary Hunton 8 July 1809,William
       Pollard sec.
Kent, Daniel m. Frances Ann Edmonds 22 May 1838
       Daniel P. Mitchell sec.
Kent, John m. Mary Mahanes 13 Dec 1800, John
       Fenla sec.
Kent, John of Northumberland County m. Nancy
       Towell 17 Apr 1809, Oliver Towles sec.
Kent, Jesse m. Fanny Brookes 18 Dec 1809, Joel
       Kent sec.

Kent, Jesse m. Harriott Hill 1 Nov 1832, Benjamin
    M. Walker sec.
Kent, Lody W. m. Caty Brooks 19 Mar 1810, Joel
    Kent sec.
Kent, Rodham m. Sally O. Stott 15 Mar 1809,Oliver
    Towles sec.
Kent, Thomas m. Priscilla Doggett 13 Feb 1795
    John Watts sec.
Kent, William m. Ann Taylor 21 Dec 1780, Elijah
    Percifull sec.
Kent, William m. Sarah Chilton 1 Sept 1787, John
    Roberts, Jr. sec.
Kent, William m. Elizabeth James, dau. Elizabeth
    James 13 July 1795, Bartley James sec.
Kent, William B. m. Jenny Lee McTyre 22 Dec 1803
    James Towles sec.
Kent, William B. m. Nancy Buchan 19 Dec 1825
    Henry E. Anderson sec.
Kern, John m. Alice H. Oliver 13 Oct 1830
    William Simmonds sec.
Kern, James m. Milly Brown 24 Dec 1817,Benjamin
    Waddey sec.
Kern, Joseph m. Annie Davis 5 Dec 1780,William
    Mason sec.
Kern, Henry, m. Joannah Robinson 23 Dec 1786
    Joseph Kern sec.
Kern, Henry m. Elizabeth Schofield 1 Dec 1788
    Joseph Kern sec.
Kernn, Burges m. Lucy Edwards 1 Feb 1803, James
    Towles sec.
Keser, Monroe m. Catherine Cox 26 Dec 1848
    James Core sec.
Kesterson, James m. Kitty Chinn Carter, dau.
    Joseph Carter 4 Feb 1801,James Towles sec.
Kesterson, James m. Kitty Chowning 16 Apr 1804
    John Chowning sec.
Kesterson, William m. Sally Kent 20 Mar 1797
    Henry Lee Gaskins sec.
Kesterson, William A. m. Eliza J. P. Mitchell
    dau. George Mitchell 13 Sept 1821,Warner
    Kent sec.
Key, George m. Jane Veney 13 Dec 1831, Spencer
    W. Pinn sec.
Key,William H. m. Polly Pinn 30 Dec 1835, John
    Hurst sec.
Kidd, Benjamin, widower m. Frances Tapscott, wid
    1 Aug 1798, William George sec.

Kidd, Robert B. m. Caroline Chowning 9 Jan 1832
Robert T. Dunaway sec.
Kirk, Anthony m. Sarah Brent 4 May 1747, Thomas
Edwards, Jr. sec.
Kirk, Anthony m. Elizabeth Fenley 19 Jan 1789
Charles Hubbard sec.
Kirk, George m. Sally Brent 20 May 1784, Thomas
Brent sec.
Kirk, James m. Mary Norris 27 Aug 1762 Charles
Bell sec.
Kirk, James, Jr. m. Lucy Carter 19 May 1768, Dale
Carter sec.
Kirk, John m. Sally Pollard 25 Feb 1801, William
Fallin sec.
Kirk, William H. m. Elizabeth M. Myers 9 Aug 1830
Charles Rogers sec.
Kirkmyer, Frederick m. Elizabeth Simlock 4 Nov 1803
Robert Daniel sec.
Kirkmyre, Frederick m. Catherine Carter 27 Apr
1831, James W. Degges sec.
Kirkmyer, George m. Catherine M. Saunders 23 Dec
1833, James Sanders sec.
Kirkham, Branton m. Sarah Hathaway 6 May 1839
William N. Kirk
Kirkham, John m. Hannah Brent 31 Dec 1802, Thomas
Pullen sec.
Kirkham, John m. Elizabeth Hill 18 Dec 1805, John
Hill sec.
Kirkham, William m. Elizabeth G. Wilson 22 Dec
1801, John Kirkham sec.
Knight, John m. Elizabeth Riveer 24 Nov 1785
Peter Riveer sec.
Knight, John m. Lucy G. Talley 4 Dec 1822, James
Robinson, Jr. sec.

Lamkin, Chattin m. Betty Miller 12 Oct 1780
Lansdale, Thomas m. Ann Miller 28 Jan 1803, John
Miller sec.
Lansdell, John m. Betsy W. Spriggs 12 July 1832
Daniel P. Mitchell sec.
Laws, William m. Louisa Lewis 3 Mar 1831, Cyrus
Nickin sec.
Lawson, Anthony m. Ann Shelton 19 July 1802
George Flowers sec.
Lawson, Epaphroditus m. Ann Thornton Longwith
19 Dec 1810, John Longwith sec.

Lawson, Henry m. Esther Chinn 21 Oct 1768, James
     Kirk, Sr. sec.

Lawson, Henry C. m. Margaret S. Lee 18 Jan 1796
     Thomas Lee sec.

Lawson, Henry B. m. Sally E. McNamara 23 Jan 1826
     Thomas L. Lawson sec.

Lawson, James m. Elizabeth Barrock 1 Sept 1847
     John K. Treakle sec.

Lawson, John m. Charlotte Ashburn, dau. Margaret
     Ashburn 27 Dec 1793, William Cornelious sec.

Lawson, John m. Mary Tunstall Digges 20 Jan 1794
     James Pollard sec.

Lawson, Thomas L. m. Judith N. Brent dau. Alice
     Brent 28 Nov 1821, John T. Degge sec.

Ledford, James of Northumberland County m. ----
     Garlington, dau. Elizabeth Garlington, 9
     Jan 1770, Richard Evers sec. (badly damaged)

Ledford, John m. Judith M. George 30 Nov 1807
     James L. Norris sec.

Lee, Charles of Northumberland County m. Elizabeth
     Pinchard 8 Nov 1721, Thomas Pinchard sec.

Lee, Charles m. Mildred Henning 19 Dec 1782
     William Kirk sec. (badly damaged)

Lee, George of Northumberland County m. Frances
     Ball 16 Feb 1787, George Yerby of Richmond
     County sec.

Lee, George G. m. Ann Mary G. Carpenter 6 Feb 1841
     W. H. Haynie sec.

Lee, John m. Mary Ball 20 Dec 1749, James Ball sec.

Lee, John L. m. Elizabeth J. Ball 17 Dec 1832, John
     Sutton sec.

Lee, Kendall of Northumberland County m. Betty
     Heale, dau. Priscilla Chinn 9 July 1749
     Thomas Edwards, Jr. sec.

Lee, Richard E. m. Letty Kelly, sister of George
     Kelly, 16 Jan 1778, James Newby sec.

Lee, Richard m. Lucy Denny 18 Sept 1783, James
     Pollard sec.

Lee, Thomas m. Elizabeth Currell 1 Feb 1780
     Nicholas Currell, Jr. sec.

Lee, Thomas m. Sally Hill 23 June 1802, Ezekiel
     G. Shearman sec.

Lee, William L. m. Judith E. Ball 27 Dec 1809
     Enock George sec.

Lee, William H. m. Harriott S. Ball 27 Nov 1828
     William W. Ball sec.

Leland, Baldwin M. m. Elizabeth Haggoman, dau.
    Mary Ann Haggoman ---- 1806, James Towles sec.
Leland, Charles, widower, m. Sarah Towles 13 Dec
    1797, James Towles sec.
Leland, Charles m. Susan C. Waddey 14 Sept 1842
    Benjamin Waddey sec.
Leland, John of Northumberland County m. Lucy Lee
    20 Jan 1762, Thomas Edwards sec.
Leland, John, Jr. m. Judith Smith 19 Oct 1775
    John Hall sec.
Leland, LeRoy P. m. Ann G. Haggoman 10 Feb 1807
    Cyrus Ball sec.
Leland, Leroy G. m. Ann N. Hubbard 30 Nov 1841
    Jesse Hubbard sec.
Lemoine, Feriol m. Fanny Mitchell 24 Aug 1803
    James Towles sec.
Lewin, Charles m. Polly Armistead Nickens 1 Jan
    1805, Dale C. Edwards sec.
Lewin, John m. Betsy Pinn 24 Mar 1819, John Pinn
    sec.
Lewin, Leroy m. Nancy Pinn, dau. Nancy Pinn 3 Feb
    1836, John Jordan sec.
Lewin, Leroy m. Arreller Weaver 19 July 1848
    Jesse Cox sec.
Lewis, John of Northumberland County m. Ann S.
    Lawson 21 Oct 1784, Charles Lee of Northum-
    berland County sec.
Lewis, William m. Anne Sharpe, dau. Sarah Bond
    7 Jan 1768, William Chowning sec.
Lightburne, Capt. Henry m. Elizabeth Currell, dau.
    George Currell, 26 Dec. 1771 Thomas Perkins
    sec.
Lightborn, William m. Darkey Bell 26 Dec 1806
    Daniel P. Mitchell sec.
Locke, Addison H. m. Mary Ann Lee dau. Arthur Lee
    24 May 1839, Robert T. Dunaway sec.
Locke, Joseph m. Molly Bean 6 July 1785, John
    Beane sec.
Locke, Ludwell L. m. Sally S. Currell 6 Mar 1827
    William Currell sec.
Longwith, John m. Elizabeth Wilder 17 June 1793
    John Watts sec.
Longwith, John m. Molly Williams 6 Oct 1818
    Samuel Treacle sec.
Longworth, Burgess m. Sally Tankersley 13 Feb
    1823, Eppa Lunsford sec.
Longworth, Burgess m. Leanna Walker 25 Feb 1834
    Thomas Smith sec.

Longworth, John m. Elizabeth James 28 Nov 1826
      David H. James sec.
Longworth, John m. Mary P. James 11 June 1840
      William W. James sec.
Longworth, William m. Harriott Trott 20 June 1828
      George L. Lee sec.
Lowry, Gawin m. Behethelan Newsom 13 Dec 1745
      Jesse Ball sec.
Lowry, Gavin m. Hannah Chowning, wid. 9 May 1777
      George Carter sec.
Lowry, John m. Betty Hill 24 Dec 1791, Thomas
      Pitman sec.
Lowry, John m. Judith Darby 24 Oct 1815, J. Towles
      sec.
Lowry, John m. Jane Stott 10 Dec 1827, John W. A.
      Edmonds sec.
Luckam, John m. Mary Bennet 4 July 1786, William
      Luckam sec.
Luckum, William m. Judith Arms 11 Aug 1789,William
      Smith sec.
Lunsford,Charles m. Elizabeth Weaver 6 Apr 1836
      James Pinn sec.
Lunsford, Edwin m. Mary Carter 11 Nov 1772
      Bridgar Hainey sec.
Lunsford, Eppaphroditus m. Chloe Yopp 5 Aug 1795
      Charles Yopp sec.
Lunsford, Eppa m. Mary Briant Warwick 11 Oct 1821
      Elias Fendly
Lunsford, John m. Sarah Ellen Carter 21 Mar 1783
      Rodham Lunsford sec.
Lunsford, John m. Lettice L. Carter 17 Nov 1817
      Benjamin Waddey sec.
Lunsford, Linton m. Frankey Carter, dau. James
      Carter, 18 Aug. 1803, Chatwin Dunaway sec.
Lunsford, Moses of Northumberland County m. Anne
      Payne 19 Feb 1762, George Payne sec.
Lunsford, Moses m. Sally Lunsford dau. John
      Lunsford 8 Jan 1811, Oliver Towles sec.
Lunsford, Moses m. Margaret Edwards 11 June 1819
      James Brent sec.
Lunsford, Rodham m. Lettice Carter 26 Feb 1774
      Henry Carter sec.
Lunsford, Rodham, Jr. m. Sally Cox, dau. Thomas
      Cox 7 July 1794, William George,son of
      Lazarus sec.
Lunsford, Warner C. m. Ann M. Doggett 6 Dec 1831
      James S. Towles sec.

Lyell, John m. Mary Tayloe 11 June 1724, Thomas
 Edwards sec.

McAdams, Joseph of Northumberland County m. Sarah
 Ann Pinckard 11 July 1744, John Graham sec.
McClanahan, Thomas H. m. Ann Hinton 28 Oct 1839
 William H. Stott sec.
McCarty, Dennis of Westmoreland County m. Sarah
 Ball, dau. William Ball 22 Sept 1724
 William Ball sec.
McCarty, Thaddeus m. Ann Chinn 19 May 1758
 William Glascock sec.
McCarty, William D. m. Frances R. Carter 23 Oct
 1818, George W. Downman sec.
McCroskey, Samuel Smith m. Charlotte Taylor 10
 Apr 1772, John Smith sec.
McKenney, John M. m. Dorcas J. Talley 14 Feb
 1843, George R. Talley sec.
McNeale, Arthur m. Elizabeth Frizell 19 Aug
 1732, John Cristy sec.
McNamara, ----- m. Winefred R. Lawson 30 Aug 1804
 Henry C. Lawson sec.
McNamara, Henry m. Rosetta Johnson 20 Dec 1830
 Thomas Schofield sec.
McNamara, John m. Salley M. Gibson 13 Jan 1817
 William Gibson sec.
McNamara, Timothy, mariner, m. Mary Lawson 5 Aug
 1796, Henry C. Lawson sec.
McNamara, Timothy m. Frances Lawson 15 July 1807
 Henry Chinn Lawson sec.
McNamara, Timothy m. Eliza L. Brent 20 Nov 1820
 George Patterson sec.
McTire, Charles L. m. Elizabeth Davenport, Philip
 Warwick sec.
McTire, John m. Sally Henning 22 May 1772, Robert
 Henning sec.
McTyre, John m. Molly Doggett 21 Nov 1782, Joseph
 Dobbs sec.
McTyre, John m. Nancy Hill 17 Dec 1825, Armistead
 J. Palmer sec.
Madison, Eldrid m. Decynthia F. Payne 20 Nov 1843
 Thomas C. Callahan sec.
Mark, William m. Betty Kern, wid. 18 Jan 1796
 Elijah Percifull sec.
Marsh, Gideon m. Nancy Percifull 12 Sept 1785
 Lott Palmer sec.
Marsh, James m. Milly Angel 17 Feb 1791, George
 George Robinson sec.

Marsh, Capt. James m. Mary Carter 3 June 1836
     Richard Towill sec.
Marsh, William m. Mildred Moon 7 Mar 1795, Edwin G.
     Thomas sec.
Marshall, Charles m. Judith Steptoe 30 Oct 1821
     George W. Downman sec.
Martin, William m. Hannah Mitchell 16 Aug 1782
     James Pinchard sec.
Mason, John, son of Alley Mason, m. Sally Jones
     12 Apr 1802, James Towles sec.
Mason, John m. Elizabeth B. Waymouth 27 Jan 1818
     Charles Yerby sec.
Mason, Peter m. Nancy Davis 19 Jan 1788, John
     Brown sec.
Mason, Peter m. Thomazin Davis 26 Aug 1789
     Rawleigh Coates sec.
Mason, Peter m. Sally Sebree 24 Dec 1800, James
     Towles sec.
Mason, Peter m. Polly Sagathy 12 Sept 1805, James
     Towles sec.
Mason, Thomas m. Margaret James 1 Oct 1790
     Thomas James sec.
Mason, Thomas m. Susannah Cornelious, wid, 19 May
     1794, George Robinson sec.
Mason, Thomas; widower, m. Nancy Stott, wid. 19
     Apr 1796, James Ewell sec.
Mason, Thomas m. Lucy H. Thrall 6 Jan 1819, John
     Mason sec.
Mason, William m. Rebecca M. James 19 Dec 1831
     James Thrall sec.
Maston, John m. Sarah Robbins 16 Mar 1840, Anthony
     M. Sanders sec.
Matthews, James L. m. Louisa A. Ball 4 Nov 1835
     Samuel Downing sec.
Maxwell, John m. Frances Brent 16 Feb 1775, David
     Currie sec.
Mealy, Jesse m. Frances E. Seebree 5 Sept 1843
     Robert Brown sec.
Merryman, Thomas m. Milly Davis, dau. Joseph Davis
     1 Aug. 1803, Walter Arms sec.
Merridith, John m. Ann S. Brent 11 Dec 1828
     William Pullin sec.
Meredith, John m. Mary Dillard 13 Dec 1782
Meredith, Maj. John m. Ann C. Towell, 18 Nov 1822
     Thomas L.Lawson sec.
Miller, James R. m. Sarah B. James 22 Feb. 1841
     William E. Flowers sec.

Miller, Peter H., son of John Miller, Sr. m. Sally
Everett Newby 23 Dec 1800, William Newby sec.

Miller, Thomas m. Sally Swanson 4 Aug 1808, Rodham
Milley sec.

Miller, William m. Martha Taylor 10 Dec 1818
William Dare sec.

Milner, Francis m. Betty Ball 9 Dec 1754, William
Ball sec.

Millham, Samuel m. Martha Gardner 8 Sept 1724
Thomas Edwards sec.

Mitchell, Daniel P. m. Catherine C. Degge 1 May
1800, James Towles sec.

Mitchell, Daniel P. m. Elizabeth George 24 Feb.
1808, Henry M. Mitchell sec.

Mitchell, Daniel P., Jr. m. Virginia P. Miller
13 Dec 1827, Nathan Spriggs sec.

Mitchell, Daniel P. m. Jane E. George 17 Nov 1837
R. T. Dunaway sec.

Mitchell, George M. m. Polly Carter 23 June 1834
Thomas P. Hill sec.

Mitchell, Henry M. m. Elizabeth Brent 7 Dec 1808
Robert F. Degge sec.

Mitchell, James m. Susanna P. Shearman, dau.
Susanna Shearman, 23 Sept 1801, Daniel P.
Mitchell sec.

Mitchell, James m. Eleanor B. Brent 13 Dec 1809
Oliver Towles sec.

Mitchell, John m. Charaty Coleman 3 Aug 1744
Anthony Sydnor sec.

Mitchell, Joseph R. m. Henrietta B. Kester, dau.
Kitty Kester, 10 Nov 1825, Benjamin M
Walker sec.

Mitchell, Richard m. Peggy Gunyon 7 Mar 1783
John Glascock sec.

Mitchell, Richard m. Dolly Degges 22 July 1800
-------- Davenport sec.

Mitchell, Richard m. Frances Stubblefield 17 Sept
1823, Williamson P. Jones sec.

Mitchell, Richard m. Frances Edwards 18 Nov 1834
Robert T. Dunaway sec.

Mitchell, Richard B. m. Tomza S. Gresham 4 Oct
1845, Samuel Gresham sec.

Mitchell, Robert the younger, m. Hannah Ball 7
Sept. 1746, Richard Selden sec.

Mitchell, Thaddeus m. Ann Mitchell 8 Nov 1804
Daniel P. Mitchell sec.

Mitchell, Thaddeus m. Elizabeth Campbell 21 Dec
1812, Henry S. Pullen sec.

Mitchell, William, m. Mary Miller 24 Nov 1769, John
      Bean sec.
Mitchell, William B. m. Margaret Downman 30 May
      1815, Joseph B. Downman sec.
Montague, James m. Elizabeth Chinn 20 June 1760
      William Montague sec.
Montague, William, son of William Montague m.
      Hannah Ball dau. Sarah Ball, 16 Oct 1727,
      John Selden sec.
Montague, William m. ---an-- Ballind--- 27 Jan
      1749, Richard Selden sec. (badly damaged)
Montague, William m. Lucy Smith 11 Dec 1772
      James Selden sec.
Montague, William m. Frances Downman 17 Mar 1801
      George McA. Brown sec.
Moore, Charles m. Nancy Percifull 21 Dec 1825
      Thomas T. Atwell sec.
Moore, John m. Ann Currell 25 Aug. 1781, William
      Hinton sec.
Moore, Reuben m. Peggy McDaniel 5 Oct 1785,
      William Carter sec.
Moore, William m. Milley Angel, wid. 22 Sept.
      1792, Epaphroditus Robinson sec.
Moore, William S. m. Lilly T. Blakemore 11 Apr.
      1836, James S. Towles sec.
Morrison, James m. Anna Crowder 4 Aug. 1802
      Joshua Crowder sec.
Mott, Joseph, Jr. m. Molly Sutton, dau. of John
      Sutton of Northumberland, 15 Oct 1798
      Peter Beane sec.
Mott, Thomas m. Winifred Doggett 21 Feb 1782
      Stephen Locke sec.
Mott, Thomas m. Betty Candiff 21 Sept 1789
      Thomas Palmer sec.
Mott, William m. Elizabeth Hubbard 9 Dec 1768
      Joseph Mott sec.
Mott, William m. Lucretia Walker 4 Mar. 1796
      William Wallace sec.
Murry, Reuben m. Sinah Palmer 10 Mar 1787
      Benjamin Palmer sec.
Murray, Reubin m. Elizabeth Pitman 10 Sept 1828
      Hiram Stonham sec.
Muse, Daniel m. Jean Robinson 16 Apr 1772, Burges
      Ball sec.
Muse, John m. Elizabeth Haydon 23 Mar 1786
      Ezekiel Haydon, Jr. sec.
Myers, George F. m. Nancy Basye 11 Dec 1820
      William Oldham sec.

Myers, Matthew m. Nancy Rivers 20 May 1790, Henry
    Hinton sec.
Myers, Thomas m. Sarah Armes 13 Mar 1793, William
    George sec.
Myers, Thomas m. Peggy Rogers 23 Feb 1796,William
    George sec.   Ann
Myers, Thomas m. Mary/Harris 20 July 1807

Nagle, Edward m. Elizabeth Hinton 20 June 1800
    Henry Hinton sec.
Nash, William m. Anne Kirk dau. Christopher Kirk
    10 Feb. 1717/18
Neale, John m. Hellen Harper 1 Oct 1751, James
    Tapscott sec.
Neale, Presley m. Elizabeth Harris 13 Aug. 1788
    George Briscoe sec.
Neale, Presley m. Polly George 29 Jan 1812
    Thomas Thrall sec.
Neale, Shopleigh m. Margaret Bell, dau. John Bell
    10 Sept 1741, Thomas Edwards sec.
Newgent, Thomas m. Caty Branan 20 Nov 1813, Opie
    Dunaway sec.
Newgent, Thomas m. Fanny Lowry 15 May 1815, John
    Lowry sec.
Newsom, Robert, Jr. m. Behethelem Jones 25 Oct
    1738, James Brent sec.
Newby, Cyrus m. Elizabeth Dunaway 15 April 1818
    Moses Robinson sec.
Newby, John m. Elizabeth Hunton dau. Thomas
    Hunton, 30 Dec 1772, Richard Payne sec.
Newby, John m. Sally Hathaway 21 Jan 1808,Charles
    Bailey sec.
Newby, Oswald, Jr. m. Mary Page Carter 20 Dec 1787
    Edward Newby sec.
Newby, Oswald, widower m. Catherine Taylor 26
    July 1792, Joseph Carter sec.
Newby, William m. Ann Miller 21 Dec 1781,John
    Miller sec.
Newby, William m. Ann Newby 15 Nov 1793, James
    Robb sec.
Norris, Eppey m. Molley Arms, dau. Janey Arms
    21 Nov 1789, John Lunsford sec.
Norris, George m. Elizabeth Ledford 3 Aug 1770
    Edwin Conway sec.
Norris, George m. Nancy Minst 19 Dec 1780
Norris, James m. Judith Mitchell, dau. William
    Mitchell, Sr. 10 Mar 1792, William Mitchell
    Jr. sec.

Norris, James, Jr. m. Elizabeth H. Davenport 1 May
1832, Thomas D. Davenport sec.

Norris, John m. Jane Camele 4 Feb 1737/8, Robert
McTyre sec.

Norris, John m. Betsey Tayloe Norris dau. Eppey
Norris, 29 May 1809, Robert M. Robertson sec.

Norris, John m. Olivia Carpenter 17 June 1816, John
Carpenter sec.

Norris, Richard m. Sarah Ann Newby 11 Jan 1791,
William Newby sec.

Norris, Richard m. Sarah Stott 19 Dec 1820, Jasper
Stott sec.

Norris, Richard m. Jane Sutton 24 Dec 1844, James
Norris sec.

Norris, Thomas m. Sarah G. Chowning 3 June 1833
John Gresham sec.

Norris, William m. Judith Horton 3 Oct 1774, Elias
Edmonds sec.

Norris, William O. m. Sarah Spilman 26 Dec 1848
Cyrus Hazard sec.

Northern, Richard m. Kitty Ann Dunaway 19 Feb
1839, Robert T. Dunaway sec.

Nichols, John m. Mary Townsend 1 Dec 1769, John
Longwith sec.

Nicken, Armistead m. Polly Weaver 21 Jan 1819
John C. Pinn sec.

Nickin, Cyrus m. Mary Ann Lewin 17 Dec 1835
Lindsey Nicken sec.

Nicken, Joseph m. Polly Wiggins 26 Jan 1821
James Brent sec.

Nicken, John, Jr. m. Ann Mills 17 Sept 1791
Richard Nicken sec.

Nicken, Linsay m. Rachel C. Veney 19 Oct 1830
John Kem sec.

Nicken, Overton m. Judith Veney 17 May 1837
Armistead Nicken sec.

Nicken, Richard m. Elizabeth Hamilton 20 Aug
1806, John Nicken sec.

Nicken, Richard m. Mary Lewin 12 Aug. 1824
Daniel P. Mitchell sec.

Nickens, Lindsey m. Manerva Collins 23 Dec 1822
Charles Lewis sec.

Nickens, Robert m. Elizabeth Gray 12 Aug 1786
John Crowder sec.

Nickins, Robert, widower, m. Nancy Howe 5 Mar
1793, James Hill sec.

Nugent, Thomas m. Judith Dunaway 15 Oct 1798
    Martin Carter sec.

Nutt, James m. Jane M. Walker 30 Nov 1835
    Benjamin M. Walker sec.

Nutt, Leroy m. Alcy T. Gallo 18 Mar 1802, George
    Smither sec.

Nutt, Robert m. Charlotte McAdam Taylor 23 Jan
    ------, James Towles sec.

Nutt, William, of Northumberland County m. Mary
    Downing 16 Nov 1769, Will: Dymer sec.

Nutt, William m. Jane Swan Brent 27 Oct 1781
    Charles Lee sec.

Nutt, William O. Nutt m. Elizabeth Chinn 6 Dec
    1798, Stokely Towles sec.

Nuttall, James m. Sarah James dau. Thomas James
    13 May 1760, Benjamin Kelly sec.

Nuttall, John m. Judith Lawson 16 Nov 1775, Henry
    Lawson sec.

Oliver, George P. m. Elizabeth Meredith 4 Dec 1807
    James Towles sec.

Oliver, Lowry m. Ellen Cammell dau. Winifred
    Cammel 28 Feb 1771, William Brumley sec.

Oliver, Mathias H. m. Polly P. Davis 8 Nov 1815
    Chattin Dunaway sec.

Oliver, Tapscott m. Winifred Lunsford 21 Mar
    1780, Thomas Oliver sec.

Oliver, Thomas m. (name not filled in) 17 Aug
    1802, William Meredith sec.

Oliver, Thomas B. m. Sally Fendla 20 Sept 1813
    Elias Fendla sec.

Oliver, Thomas B. m. Sally T. Schofield 28 Nov
    1821, John Degge sec.

Oliver, Thomas R. M. m. Ann C. Beane, dau Armon
    Beane, 13 Jan 1848, Thomas Davis sec.

Oldham, Samuel m. Ann Shearman 2 Feb 1803, James
    Mitchell sec.

Oldham, Thomas m. Mary J. Blakemore 2 Jan 1839
    Thomas C. Callahan sec.

Oldham, William m. Frances Blakey 23 July 1817
    J. Towles sec.

Opie, Linsoy m. Sarah Heale dau. George Heale
    10 Feb 1734/5, Thomas Edwards sec.

Orrens, Thomas M. m. Judy Cundiff, dau. John
    Cundiff, 18 Feb. 1818, James Brent sec.

Orrill, William m. Polly Simmonds Lowry 11 Dec
    1817, John Lawson sec.

Osbourne, John m. Rebecca Bourke, dau. Marcy Bourke
    21 July 1801, James Towles sec.
Owens, William m. Frances L. Anderson 26 1832
    Edwin Lee sec.

Pace, George D. m. Elizabeth L. Hutchings 20 Oct
    1834, Richard Hutchings sec.
Pace, William K. m. Ann Chowning 3 Mar 1835
    Richard Hutchings sec.
Page, Man m. Judith Carter, dau. Robert Carter
    Consent of Robert Carter dated 26 July 1718
Palmer, Benjamin m. Polly George 30 May 1805
    Robert D. Palmer sec.
Palmer, Benjamin m. Mary George 27 Feb 1817,William
    F. Yerby sec.
Palmer, Charles m. Elizabeth Gresham 8 June 1819
    Armistead J. Palmer sec.
Palmer, John m. Lucy White 1 Oct 1787, John Gordon
    sec.
Palmer, John m. Mary Norris 19 June 1796, Eppey
    Norris sec.
Palmer, Lott m. Nancy Walker 26 Sept 1785,Thomas
    Everitt sec.
Palmer, Lott, widower, m. Betty Carter 25 July 1792
    Thomas Palmer sec.
Palmer, Lott m. Betsy Swanson 12 Mar 1807, Robert
    D. Palmer sec.
Palmer, Rawleigh m. Sally Palmer 17 Apr 1805
    Abner Palmer sec.
Palmer, Robert D. m. Milly Cundiff, dau. Richard
    & Susanna Cundiff, born January,1776, 22
    Aug. 1797, Henry Hudson sec.
Palmer, Robert D. m. Dolly J. Palmer 21 Dec 1807
    Lott Palmer sec.
Palmer, Thomas m. Judith Cundiff 29 July 1785
    John Cundiff sec.
Palmer, Thomas D. m. Ann Knight 29 July 1847
    George Talley sec.
Parrott, George W. m. Elizabeth Robertson 24 Apr
    1811, George Robertson sec.
Pasquit, John m. Elizabeth Newby 2 Oct 1797
    Oswald Newby sec.
Payne, Edward m. Sally Davenport 12 Nov 1795
    Thomas Chowning sec.
Payne, Edward m. Appia Palmer 11 Aug 1814,James
    Towles sec.
Payne, Edward m. Elizabeth Fendley 22 Nov 1843
    Thomas Payne sec.

Payne, George m. Frances Edmunds 13 Oct 1729
Thomas Edwards sec.

Payne, George m. Polly Smith Doggett dau. John
Doggett, 14 Sept 1815, Richard Payne sec.

Payne, George W. m. Esther C. Lawson, dau. Margaret
Lawson, 20 Apr 1835, James Harding sec.

Payne, Col. John m. Jean Chichester 20 June 1757
George Heale sec.

Payne, John m. Ellen Payne 30 Mar 1770, Benjamin
Waddy, Jr. sec.

Payne, John m. Bridget Blakemore dau. Edward
Blakemore, 17 July 1771, Thomas Shearman sec.

Payne, John m. Harriott Eustace 29 Apr 1818
Richard Payne sec.

Payne, Merriman, son of Joseph Payne m. Catherine
Brent 19 Aug 1734, Hugh Brent sec.

Payne, Richard m. Ellen Bailey 20 Jan 1764, James
Ball sec.

Payne, Richard m. Alice Shearman dau. Ann Shearman
21 Jan 1773, Elias Edmonds sec.

Payne, Thomas m. Catherine Currell 3 Mar 1839, James
A. Palmer sec.

Payne, William m. Lucy George 16 July 1762, Charles
Rogers sec.

Payne, William, son of Richard H. Payne, m. Sarah
Ann Taylor 16 Dec 1807, Thomas Taylor sec.

Payne, William J. m. Elizabeth Chowning 30 Nov
1815, James Towles sec.

Peirce, Joseph m. Alice M. Tapscott 2 Nov 1830
Richard B. Hutt sec.

Peirce, Stephen Scranton m. Doratha Hinton 14 May
1800, Henry Hinton sec.

Pemberton, Larkin m. Mary Newby, dau. Oswald Newby
7 Oct 1788, Oswald Newby sec.

Pendleton, James, of King & Queen County m. Mary
Lyell, wid. 8 Jan 1727/8, Samuel Ball sec.

Percifull, Edward m. Alice DeSelvey 26 June 1820
Richard Payne sec.

Percifull, Edward m. Nancy C. Simmonds 27 Feb
1833, William Simmonds sec.

Percifull, Elijah m. Betsy Carter 17 Mar 1787
Isaac Taylor sec.

Percifull, Elijah m. Elizabeth Rivers Davis 16
Jan 1797, Presley Cockerill sec.

Percifull, John Y. m. Margaret Dunaway 11 Apr 1812
J. Towles sec

Percifull, Robert m. Nancy Sutton 29 Dec 1812
Thomas Potts sec.

Perkins, Thomas m. Ellinor Currell 22 Mar 1735/6
    Isaac Currel sec.

Perkins, Capt. Thomas m. Sarah Ann Currell, 16 Dec
    1771, Merriman Payne sec.

Phillips, Bryan m. Elizabeth Stott 16 Nov 1724
    James Stott sec.

Phillips, Bernard m. Sarah Towell 2 Apr 1823, John
    Gresham sec.

Phillips, George m. Mary Yerby, dau. Elizabeth
    Woodbridge, 3 Sept 1765, William Chilton sec.

Phillips, William m. Ellen Carter 18 May 1790
    Joseph Carter sec.

Phlippin, Humphrey m. Molly Cox 7 Apr 1806 ------
    Currell sec.

Picknon, George, of Northumberland County m. Mary
    Billings 6 Oct 1787, James Wallace sec.

Pierce, Daniel m. Nancy Robins 22 Feb 1826, Jasper
    Stott sec.

Pierce, Randall, of Westmoreland County m. Ann
    Graham, 1 Dec 1794, Bryant Phillips sec.

Pinn, Aaron m. Mary Kelly Weaver 3 Mar 1794
    Spencer Weaver sec.

Pinn, Aaron m. Lucy Tankersley 15 Mar 1847, James
    Pinn sec.

Pinn, Benjamin m. Betty Bell, dau. Elias Bell 1
    Apr. 1791, Richard Nickens sec.

Pinn, James m. Dorcus Oliver 21 Jan 1834, John
    Lewin sec.

Pin, Robin m. Sally Wood 25 Apr 1789, Benjamin
    Pin sec.

Pinn, Robert m. Mary Casely? 19 Apr 1803, Aaron
    Pinn sec.

Pinn, Robert m. Roxy Thomas 23 Feb 1831, John C
    Pinn sec.

Pinn, William m. Winney Hill 26 Dec 1825, John
    Lewin sec.

Pinckard, Edward m. Nancy Meredith 24 Aug 1805
    Dale C. Edwards sec.

Pinckard, Edward m. Elizabeth Branberry 2 Nov
    1813, George M. Mitchell sec.

Pinckard, Thomas m. Ann H. Pollard 17 Jan 1842
    Samuel Gresham sec.

Pitman, Burges m. Molly P. Jopes ----------
    Elijah Percifull sec.

Pitman, Edward C. m. Mary Rosson 4 Dec 1817
    Charles Taylor sec.

Pitman, Elismon m. Sarah Ann Sebree 12 Apr 1824
Cornelius Sullivant sec.
Pitman, George, widower, m. Judith Clark, wid. 1
Jan 1805, Moses Robinson sec.
Pitman, George m. Alice T. George 11 Jan 1826
William T. Jessee sec.
Pitman, Isaac m. Margaret James 26 May 1768
John James sec.
Pitman, Isaac, widower m. Sally White 15 Oct 1792
Fortunatus Pitman sec.
Pitman, Isaac m. Malinda Hathaway 4 Jan 1818
Andrew Chilton sec.
Pitman, James m. Nancy Webb 17 Dec 1792, Lett:
Palmer sec.
Pitman, Jeduthun m. Caty Webb 29 Mar 1783
Harrice Webb sec.
Pitman, Jesse m. Elizabeth Evins 24 Dec 1835
Richard L. Dozier sec.
Pitman, Leroy M. m. Roxy Kemm 29 Dec 1825, John
Fawcett sec.
Pitman, Leroy M. m. Margaret Eaton 20 Aug 1828
Robert Dunaway sec.
Pitman, Richard m. Lyddy Briscoe 20 Mar 1788
William Warren sec.
Pitman, Thomas m. Polly Roberts 30 Mar 1786
John Roberts sec.
Pitman, Thomas m. Frances Hill 6 Jan 1791
Charles Brent sec.
Pitman, Thomas m. Nancy Forester 22 Dec 1803
Robert Forester sec.
Pitman, Thomas m. Cyntha Hathaway 25 Aug 1807
William Brent sec.
Pitman, Thomas m. Emily M. Doggett 25 Dec 1839
Robert H. Smith sec.
Pitman, William m. Elizabeth Hill 4 Nov 1801
John Hill sec.
Pitman, William m. Polly Dodson 11 Jan 1809
John C. Hinton sec.
Pitman, William m. Lidda R. Beane 24 Nov 1809
John Bean sec.
Pollard, James m. Catherine Payne Brent 28 Sept
1818, Hiram Carpenter sec.
Pollard, William m. Betty Brent, orphan of Hugh
Brent, 22 Mar 1762, Whaley Newby sec.
Pollard, William m. Nancy A. George 21 Aug 1797
John Steptoe sec.
Pope, George m. Fanny McTire 24 Mar 1796, Charles
L. McTire sec.

Pope, Leroy m. Elizabeth Mitchell 24 Apr 1765
    James Tapscott sec.
Pope, Nicholas m. Elizabeth Fleet dau. John Fleet
    22 Jan 1772, Jesse Robinson sec.
Porter, William m. Elizabeth H. Brent 12 Jan 1833
    James Chowning sec.
Pott, Francis B. m. Judith Coates 27 Nov 1813
    Spencer Watts sec.
 Potts, John m. Sally Chowning 13 May 1802
    Thomas Potts sec.
Potts, Thomas m. Ann Merryman 20 Apr 1786,Joseph
    Fielding sec.
Powell, William m. Nancy Stepto 10 Oct 1762,John
    Stepto sec.
Prichard, Thomas m. Ann Corbin Griffin 17 June
    1784, David Currie sec.
Pullen, George m. Sally Warwick 1 Jan 1816,Thomas
    Coates sec.
Pullen, Henry m. Hannah Rogers 11 Dec 1782,George
    Cammell sec.
Pullen, Jeduthun m. Jane Claughton 9 Jan 1796
    Jonathan Pullen sec.
Pullen, John B. m. Sally B. Currell 4 Apr 1825
    James Hammond sec.
Pullen, Jonathan m. Betty Anne Brumley dau.
    Samuel Brumley, 16 Dec 1763, William Brumley
    sec.
Pullen, Jonathan of Richmond County m. Betsey L.
    Cannon 17 Jan 1795, Jeduthin Pullen of Richmond
    County sec.
Pullen, Lindsey m. Judith Barret Dameron 15 Jan
    1801, John Tapscott sec.
Pullen, Thaddeus, widower,m. Frances Frizel
    Meredith 16 Oct 1797, William Meredith sec.
Pullen, William m. Molly Luckham 19 Mar 1811
    John Hathaway sec.
Pullin, Thaddeus m. Nancy Fiendly 4 May 1793,John
    Pullin sec.
Pullin, William m. Hannah Baylie 17 Nov 1791
    William Brumley sec.
Pullin, William m. Amelia Snow 17 Dec 1821,George
    F.Myers sec.
Pullin, William m. Judith C. Fendle 24 Jan 1844
    Isaac Pitman sec.
Pursley, Joseph C. m. Polly Hutchings 10 May 1831
    Augustus G. Parker sec.

Rain, Samuel m. Hagar Davis dau. John Davis 21 Dec
1723, Richard Curtis sec.

Rains, Rawleigh m. Peggy Reveer 24 Sept 1791, Peter
Reveer sec.

Rains, William m. Nancy M Norris 31 Dec 1821 John
Norris sec.

Ready, Daniel m. Kitty Brown 16 Jan 1806, Presley
Cockrill sec.

Reaves, John m. Nancy Davis 27 Mar 1786, Joshua
Crowder sec.

Reaves, Nicholas m. Levinia H. Lawson 17 July 1799
James Towles sec.

Reaves, William m. Jane Alford 5 July 1833, Thomas
Schofield sec.

Redwood, William H m. Catherine C. Chowning 2 Sept
1843, James Chowning sec.

Reeves, Eaton m. Priscilla Palmer 14 Aug 1724
William Reeves of Northumberland County sec.

Rees, Daniel m. Alice Williams 25 Dec 1809, George
Wale sec.

Revere (Riveer), John W. m. Nancy D. Kirk 16 July
1804, William Kirk sec.

Rice, John m. Betsy Gerrard 18 Dec 1799, James
Bush sec.

Rice, Peter W. m. Elizabeth Sampson -- Jan 1838
Thomas K Robinson sec.

Rice, Thomas m. Nancy C. Hazzard 6 Mar 1838,
Richard D. Routt sec.

Rich, David m. Hannah Jones 12 Aug 1786, Peter
Hard sec.

Rich, Robert m. Polly Wood 2 Nov 1813, Charles
Wood sec.

Rich, Robert m. Darrina Laws 26 Dec 1827
Armistead Nicken sec.

Rich, Thadeus m. Judith Nicken 14 May 1828
Armistead Nicken sec.

Richards, John m. Mary Hunton 31 Dec 1777, John
Newby sec.

Richards, Lewis m. Lucy Hunton dau. Thomas
Hunton, 6 May 1788, Mark Towell sec.

Richardson, John m. Mary Wilson 29 Oct 1784
George Pitman sec.

Riveer (Revere) Cyrus m. Mary Pittman 13 Nov
1826, John T. Degges sec.

Riveer, John m. Mary Lawson 17 Dec 1771, William
Edwards sec.

Riveer, Joel m. Betsey 4 Mar 1817, Robert D.Palmer
        sec.
Riveer, Richard m. Margaret Brent 1 Oct 1787
        Thomas Hubbard sec.
Robb, James m. Frances Buckles 9 Jan 1733, John
        Buckles sec.
Rob, James m. Judith Carter, wid. 7 Jan 1794
        Henry Pullin sec.
Robb, James m. Caty Bailey 22 Dec 1803, John Robb
        sec.
Robins, Archibald m. Mary Meredith, wid. 20 Apr
        1797, John Hammond sec.
Robins, Elijah m. Priscilla Robinson 19 Sept 1803
        Jesse Robinson sec.
Robins, Jesse m. Alice Burgess Hinton 21 Apr 1800
        Henty Hinton sec.
Robbins, John m. Sarah Hinton dau. Arch^d: Hinton
        6 Mar 1838, John Maston sec.
Roberts, John m. Elizabeth Mahone 4 Feb 1780
        David Garland sec.
Roberts, John m. Mary Longwith 16 July 1787
        William Kirk sec.
Roberts, John m. Caty George 6 Mar 1811, Bailey
        George sec.
Roberts, John m. Mary A. Wilder 1 Dec 1825,
        Michael Wilder sec.
Roberts, Joseph G. m. Henrietta Berry Mitchell
        27 Feb 1816, Thomas Norris sec.
Robertson, Andrew m. Ellen Chichester 27 Nov
        1758, Edward Ker sec.
Robertson, Andrew m. Catherine L. Brent 3 May
        1809 Robert D. Palmer sec.
Robertson, Andrew m. Sidney T. Hathaway 20 Apr
        1835, John Currell sec.
Robertson, Robert M. m. Jane Newton Brent 28 Jan
        1800, James Towles sec.
Robertson, Thomas G. m. Lettice L. Brent 11 Dec
        1801, John Steptoe sec.
Robinson, Cyrus m. Lucy Alford 31 Dec 1811, Moses
        Robinson sec.
Robinson, Epaphroditus m. Milly Chilton, 22 July
        1785, James Tapscott sec.
Robinson, Epaphroditus m. Betsey Moireson 9 May
        1800, Presley Cockerill sec.
Robinson, James m. Winnie Taff 20 Mar 1786
        George Robinson sec.

Robinson, James, Jr. m. Lucinda G. Thrailkill 23
        Oct 1810, Thomas Beane, Jr. sec.
Robinson, Jesse, of Northumberland m. Lucy Rob 21
        May 1764, Moses Lunsford sec.
Robinson, Jesse m. Peggy Norris 14 Jan 1779
        Martin Norris sec.
Robinson, Jesse, the younger, m. Polly Coffee 27
        Apr 1787, Thomas Routt sec.
Robinson, Josiah m. Maria Brown 7 Feb. 1839, Travis
        Sebree sec.
Robinson, Joel m. Emily Cundiff 16 May 1836, Isaac
        Cundiff sec.
Robinson, John m. Margaret Reid 30 Oct 1773, Thomas
        Shearman sec.
Robinson, Moses m. Fanny Robinson 8 Jan 1791
        Epaphroditus Robinson sec.
Robinson, Moses m. Betsey Kernn, grandaughter of
        James Towles, 3 May 1807, Edward Payne sec.
Robinson, Moses m. Fanny Dunnaway 29 May 1817
Robinson, Moses m. Beheathaland N. George 8 Aug
        1828, Edward Payne sec.
Robinson, William M. m. Nancy Sullivant 24 Jan
        1797, Samuel Garnet sec.
Robinson, William m. Margarett Sullivan 11 Dec
        1833, Josiah Robinson sec.
Rock, Charles m. Winnifred Lee 13 Sept 1796, George
        Dodson sec.
Roderick, Anthony m. Elizabeth Reaves 16 Feb 1786
        John Fleet sec.
Rogers, Charles m. Catherine Brent 20 Mar 1762
        William Sydnor sec.
Rogers, Charles m. Peggy Chowning 15 Apr 1775
        William Chowning sec.
Rogers, Charles m. Judith Hathaway 3 Mar 1796
        Joseph Carter sec.
Rogers, Charles m. Mary Ann Y. Myers 2 Feb 1827
        Fauntleroy N. Chilton sec.
Rogers, Charles m. Margaret Ann Chilton 9 July
        1832, William H. Kirk sec.
Rogers, Charles m. Elizabeth Ann Saunders 4 May
        1839, William Saunders sec.
Rogers, Edward, of Northumberland County, m.
        Katherine Edmonds 21 Sept 1750, John Stott
        sec.
Rogers, John m. Jane Walters 23 Aug 1723, John
        Callehan sec.
Rogers, John m. Olivia Norris 7 Dec 1827, John
        Kemm sec.

Rogers, John m. Lavania T. Hudson 6 May 1848, H.B.
    Scott sec.
Rogers, William H. m. Mary Page Carter, dau.Joseph
    Carter, Jr. 9 Dec 1813, Merryman Chilton sec.
Row, William C. m. Ann Lee 1 Apr 1796, Henry C.
    Lawson sec.
Rowe, William m. Sarah Ann Garner, dau. Griffin
    Garner, 11 Jan 1847, Joseph Evans sec.
Rowand, Thomas m. Mary Kenner, dau. Brerreton
    Kenner, 27 Aug 1771, Edwin Conway sec.

Sampson, John m. Molly Cundiff 20 Apr 1808,George
    Smither sec.
Sanders, Anthony m. Judith A. Currell 28 Mar 1836
    William C. Currell sec.
Sanders, John W. m. Lucy F. E. Cox, dau. John G.
    Cox, 3 Oct 1846, James R. Sanders sec.
Saunders, Presly m. Winny Kent 18 Sept 1783
    Thomas Hubbard sec.
Saunders, Richard m. Alice M. Chilton 9 Mar 1835
    Raw: W. Chilton sec.
Saunders, William m. Harriott Kirk 23 Nov 1820
    Joseph Norris sec.
Schofield, Henry m. Polly Tapscott 26 Dec 1803
    Thomas Schofield sec.
Schofield, Sharpley m. Ann M. E. Ashbourn, dau.
    James Ashbourn, 7 Jan 1834, Thomas Smither
    sec.
Schofield, Thomas m. Catherine George, dau.
    Catherine George 5 Apr 1792, Richard Yerby
    sec.
Schofield, Thomas m. Betsey Clayton 20 June 1796
    Fortunatus George sec.
Schofield, Thomas m. Lucy Hinton 9 Feb 1831
    Henry L. McNamara sec.
Schofield, William, son of William Schofield, m.
    Judith Purcell, 9 Jan 1762, John Kent, Jr.
    sec.
Scott, Thomas m. Susanna Odor 22 Apr 1730,Thomas
    Edwards sec.
Scrosby, James, of Middlesex County, m. Elizabeth
    Lee 15 Apr 1737, Richard Martin sec.
Scrimger, William m. Alice B. Williams 1 June
    1825, Peter Williams sec.
Scurlock, George, Jr. m. Frankey Boid 14 Jan 1791
    Henry Hazard sec.
Sebree, Henry B. m. Elizabeth Cundiff, dau. John
    Cundiff 14 Nov 1821, Isaac Cundiff sec.

Sebree, James m. Delia G. Davis 20 Apr 1829,Richard
    Davis sec.
Sebree, Jesse m. Delilah Revier 26 Sept 1796, Jery
    Nash sec.
Sebree, John m. Mary Frazer 19 June 1797, Rawleigh
    Tapscott sec.
Sebree, Joseph m. Frances Thrift, 20 May 1836,John
    Thrift sec.
Sebree, Moses m. Pharmelia Davis 21 July 1834
    Francis Sebree sec.
Sebree, Nicholas m. Betty Barns Marsh 17 Dec 1798
    Lot Palmer sec.
Sebree, Tarpley m. Hannah Thomas 20 Mar 1798,James
    Robb sec.
Sebree, Traves m. Dealy Church 22 Dec 1823, Moses
    Robinson sec.
Sebrey, John m. Peggy Dudley 8 Mar 1826, Joel
    Riveer sec.
Sebrey, Robert m. Winney Ann Sebrey 13 May 1829
    Robert L. Brent sec.
Selbey, William m. Elizabeth Fleming 5 Feb 1807
    William Fleming sec.
Selbeay, William m. Lucy Chilton, dau. Thomas &
    Jamima Chilton, now Jamima Cox, wife of
    Thomas Cox, 30 Aug 1794, Edward Chilton sec.
Selden, James m. Mildred Ball dau. Joseph Ball, 7
    May 1766, Thomas Winder Ewell sec.
Selden, John, of Elizabeth City County, m. Sarah
    Ball, dau. Richard Ball, 14 Oct 1725, David
    Ball sec.
Selden, Richard, son of John Selden, m. Mary Ball,
    dau. James Ball, 21 Oct 1741
Selden, Richard m. Elizabeth Nutt 14 June 1803
    James Towles sec.
Settle, William m. Nancy Blakemore 29 1794,William
    Chowning sec.
Settle, William m. Mary Chowning 13 Feb 1819, John
    S. Chowning sec.
Settle, William m. Lucy Payne 27 Dec 1819, Stephen
    Freeman sec.
Seward, John m. Elizabeth Chinn 3 Sept 1806
    Chichester Tapscott sec.
Seward, John, widower, m. Frances Lee 28 May 1829
    Joseph W. Chinn sec.
Shackelford, Edwin m. Elizabeth Peirce, dau. L.
    Peirce, 27 Sept 1845, William M. James sec.
Shay, Martin m. Penelope Pursell, dau. Joseph R.
    Pursell, 7 Jan 1840, Henry Shay sec.

Shelton, John P. m. Sally M. C. George 15 Jan 1823
    Michael W. George sec.

Shelton, Newman m. Lucinda Spilman 25 Jan 1819
    Jesse Hammond sec.

Shelton, Richard S. m. Nancy Kent 24 Sept 1788
    Elias Schofield sec.

Shelton, Thomas m. Caty Payne dau. Bridget Payne
    22 Apr 1790, Edward Blakemore sec.

Shearman, Ezekiel G. m. Betsey Tapscott 14 July
    1808, Martin Shearman sec.

Shearman, Ezekiel G. m. Elizabeth M. R. James 27
    May 1846, John S. Currell sec.

Shearman, Joseph m. Susanna Chinn, sister of
    Robert Chinn, 10 Mar 1768, Bridgar Haynie
    sec.

Shearman, Joseph m. Lavinia Shearman 10 Feb 1805
    Ezekiel G. Shearman sec.

Shearman, Joseph m. Betsey M. Steptoe 7 Apr 1807
    Enock George sec.

Shearman, Joseph m. Caroline Meredith 2 Mar 1819
    Charles Taylor sec.

Shearman, Martin m. Mary Hunt, dau. Elizabeth
    Stott, 7 Jan 1762, Christopher Bayles sec.

Shearman, Martin m. Alice Tapscott 23 Feb 1784
    Rawh: Tapscott sec.

Shearman, Rawleigh m. Elizabeth Gilbert, orphan
    of Ezekiel Gilbert, dec. 29 June 1756
    Maurice Gilbert sec.

Shearman, Samuel M. m. Nancy Martin 5 Oct 1801
    Hugh Brent sec.

Shearman, Thomas m. Molly Bailey 7 June 1794
    Rawleigh Tapscott sec.

Shearman, Thomas m. Elizabeth Mitchell 17 Dec
    1817, Spencer George sec.

Shearlock, Richard m. Ann Pinn 17 Nov 1794, John
    Chowning sec.

Sherbourne, Hugh S. m. Joanna Hutchinson, wid.
    18 Mar 1794, Samuel Elgar sec.

Short, Moses m. Elizabeth Mahnes, dau. Elizabeth
    Mahnes 17 May 1817, Onesephrosefrus Harvey
    sec.

Short, Thomas m. Liddy Carter, dau. Ann Carter 7
    Jan 1788, John Carter sec.

Short, Thomas m. Elizabeth Cox 20 July 1801
    James Towles sec.

Short, Thomas m. Elizabeth Cox 23 Oct 1830
    Edward Percifull sec.

Sibruk, John Y. m. Elizabeth A. Towles 22 May
    1847, James Ingram sec.

Sidner, Eppa m. Jane Nickins 16 Feb 1848, Robert
    Nickins sec.
Simes, James m. Eliza Haydon 21 Apr 1834, Joseph
    S. Haydon sec.
Sims, William m. Rathey Percifull 25 June 1804
    Robert D. Palmer sec.
Simmons, James m. Elizabeth Hammonds 3 Jan 1767
    Thomas Hammonds sec.
Simmonds, Charles m. Lucy T. George 21 Jan 1811
    Thomas Thrall sec.
Simmonds, Charles m. Susan Kemm 20 Dec 1832, John
    E. Kemm sec.
Simmonds, Charles m. Sarah Brent 26 Dec 1839
    George Brent sec.
Simmonds, John m. Sinah Mahams dau. Meredith
    Mahams, 8 Apr 1799, James Simmonds sec.
Simmonds, William m. Frances Robb sec. 17 Aug
    1801; Chatten Dunaway sec.
Slaughter, Roston m. Lucy Haydon 19 July 1824
    Wickliffe George sec.
Smallwood, John m. Lucy Fleet 16 June 1781,Henry
    Fleet sec.
Smith, Baldwin Mathews, of Northumberland County,
    m. Frances Burges 2 Dec 1748,Thomas Edwards
    sec.
Smith, Rev. Charles, of Northumberland County m.
    Elizabeth Chilton -- Feb 1728/9, Thomas
    Edwards sec.
Smith, George m. Milly Merryman 23 Sept 1813
    William Smith sec.
Smith, Gilbert m. Rocksey Clarke 25 Feb 1835
    John Hurst sec.
Smith, John m. Ann Neasum 23 Mar 1754, William
    Stamps sec.
Smith, John Matthews m. Sarah Chinn 20 Sept 1791
    Joseph Chinn sec.
Smith, John m. Margarett Ann Boatman, dau. John
    Boatman 8 Feb 1846, Joseph Tapscott sec.
Smith, Robert H. m. Catherine L. Hunt, dau.
    Lucinda L. Hunt 24 Nov 1840, William T.
    Dalby sec.
Smith, Robert H. m. Catherine George, dau. Zamoth
    George 25 Feb 1846, Robert Edmonds sec.
Smither, George m. Ann F. Spiller 14 Jan 1805
    Benedictus Spiller sec.
Smither, John m. Lucy Carter, dau. Thomas Carter
    11 Nov 1761, Bridgar Haynie sec.
Smither, William m. Elizabeth Lawson 5 Aug 1803
    Henry C. Lawson sec.

Smock, James m. Sarah Hunton 30 Mar 1787, Joseph
    Saunders sec.
Snail, Capt. Thomas m. Elizabeth Weathers Haynes,
    orphan of James Haynes, dec. 26 July 1762,
    Charles Bell sec.
Snow, John m. Lucy Garton 2 May 1808, James
    Morrison sec.
Sorrell, Edward, of Northumberland County, m.
    Darcris Lewin 15 Dec 1814, Richard Nicken sec.
Sorrell, Martin m. Judith Causy 14 Dec 1819
    Edward Sorrell sec.
Spann, John T. m. Elisabeth A. Doggett 22 Aug
    1836, William H. Carter sec.
Spilman, George m. Alice Yopp, 23 May 1808, Thomas
    Haydon sec.
Spilman, Joshua m. Mary Ayliff 1 Apr 1779, Isaac
    Currell sec.
Spilman, Joshua, widower m. Barbary Dameron, wid.
    6 Feb. 1794, Bartlet Overstreet sec.
Spilman, Stokely J. m. Lucy B. Chilton, dau.
    Lucinda Chilton 22 Apr 1841, Michael Wilder
    sec.
Spilman, William m. Elizabeth Lunsford 22 Dec
    1803, James Towles sec.
Spilman, William m. Elizabeth Greenwood 2 Feb
    1835, Anthony M. Sanders sec.
Spriggs, Ephraim, brother of Nathan Spriggs m.
    Lucy Flower, wid. 1 Oct 1787, Thomas Hubbard
    sec.
Spriggs, Ephraim m. Sarah Hammond 18 Jan 1802
    James Towles sec.
Spriggs, Joseph m. Winney Spriggs, dau Nathan
    Spriggs, 27 Dec 1824, James Nutt sec.
Spriggs, Nathan m. Sarah Hutchings 2 June 1788
    George W. Yerby sec.
Spriggs, Nathan m. Nancy Spriggs 21 May 1829
    Richard W. H. Brent sec.
Stamps, William m. Ellinor Brent, Jr., Dau.
    Catherine Brent 5 Nov 1750, Robert Edwards
    & Jesse Carter sec.
Steptoe, John m. Joanna Lawson, dau. Jean
    Lawson, consent of Jean Lawson dated 10
    June 1727
Steptoe, John m. Elizabeth Martin George 12 Dec.
    1786, James Pollard sec.
Stepto, William, of Northumberland County m.
    Betty Woodbridge Yerby, dau. George 4 Jan
    1764, John Kent, Jr. sec.

Steptoe, William m. Joanna Doggett 5 Oct 1772
    Robert Chinn sec.

Stevens, Christopher m. Mary Armes 21 Feb 1717/18
    William Cornelius sec.

Stephens, George, of Orange County m. Priscilla
    Brent 15 Oct 1787, Joseph Steptoe sec.

Stephens, George m. Elizabeth B. George 25 Jan
    1819, Spencer George sec.

Stephens, John m. Elizabeth Cornelious, dau.
    William Cornelious, 23 Mar 1789, William
    Sullivan sec.

Stephens, Joseph m. Charlotte Brent 15 Mar 1782
    Newton Brent sec.

Stephens, Joseph G. m. Margaret Peirce 27 May
    1848, William Pollard sec.

Stephens, Richard m. Frances Payne, dau. George
    Payne, 20 Dec 1756, George Payne, Jr. sec.

Stephens, Richard m. Frances Mott 19 Dec 1808
    Peter Beane sec.

Stephens, Richard A. m. Alcinda M. Wooddy 29 Nov
    1822, Addison Hall sec.

Stephens, William E. m. Catherine Minter 7 May
    1824, David H. James sec.

Stonham, Hiram m. Mary B. Yerby 10 Apr 1828
    Opie Beane sec.

Stoncham, Samuel m. Elizabeth R. Palmer 3 Dec
    1817, Robert D. Palmer sec.

Stott, Bartholomew m. Elizabeth Fallin 20 Mar
    1729, Thomas Beane sec.

Stott, Jasper m. Mary Ann Miller 11 Nov 1822

Stott, Jasper m. Elizabeth Yerby 22 May 1826
    Benjamin M Walker sec.

Stott, John S. m. Alcy Davis 1 May 1813, Richard
    Davis sec.

Stott, John S. m. Rebeckah M. Thrall 1 June 1816
    Calvin George sec.

Stott, Oliver m. Molly Harris 25 Dec 1780, George
    Nash sec.

Stott, Oliver m. Elizabeth Norris 19 Sept 1786
    Jereboam Howard sec.

Stott, Richard m. Nanny Bush 19 Oct 1786, William
    Luckam sec.

Stott, Richard m. Polly C. Newsom 9 July 1804
    Thomas Flint sec.

Stott, Thomas m. Betty Stonham 18 Mar 1765
    Richard Mitchell sec.

Stott, William m. Sarah F. Hinton 19 Apr 1797
    Henry Hinton sec.

Stott, William H. m. Fanny B. Mitchell 20 Dec 1830
Jasper Stott sec.

Strachan, Robert G. m. Eliza H. A. Currie dau. E.
Currie. 26 Mar 1821, Ellyson Currie sec.

Strother, George m. Sarah S. Chowning 20 Nov 1834
James Chowning sec.

Sullivan, Cornelius m. Mary Sampson 23 Dec 1833
Robert F. Dunaway sec.

Sullivan, James V. m. Ann Flower 20 Feb 1843, Allen
D. Reade sec.

Sullivan, Robert m. Elizabeth Dunaway 11 June 1845
Martin Shay sec.

Sullivan, William m. Elizabeth Fendley 11 Oct 1790
William Cornelious sec.

Sullivan, William, widower, m. Caty Ward, wid. 2
July 1794, John Digges sec.

Sullivant, Thomas m. Nancy Stoneham 23 Feb 1808
William Sullivant sec.

Sullivant, John m. Mary Nichols 2 July 1779, William
Doggett sec.

Sullivant, Thomas, of Northumberland County, m.
Sally Cundiff, dau. John Cundiff, 12 July 1815
John M. Robb sec.

Summers, Hugh m. Sarah Ann Hammond, dau. William
Hammond, 28 Dec 1836, Thomas Martin sec.

Sutton, James, son of Moses Sutton m. Mary Cundiff
24 Sept 1792, Abner Palmer sec.

Sutton, Samuel m. Winifred Cundiff 19 Jan 1787,
Isaac Taylor sec.

Swain, William m. Charlotte Sebree 16 Feb 1796,
John Hammonds sec.

Swain, William m. Catherine Talley 28 Jan 1822,
Elisman Pitman sec.

Swanson. Asa, widower m. Betty H. Garton, dau.
Milley Garton, 8 July 1791, Thomas Mott sec.

Sydnor, Anthony, son of William & Catherine Sydnor
m. Elizabeth Taylor 3 Jan 1736/7, Thomas
Edwards sec.

Sydnor, Anthony m. Elizabeth Hinton 1 Jan 1788
William Hinton, Jr. sec.

Sydnor, Anthony m. Elizabeth Chowning 7 Jan 1788
William Chowning sec.

Sydnor, Fortunatus m. Elizabeth Thorpe 8 June 1765
Thomas Shearman sec.

Sydnor, Joseph m. Ann Chowning, dau. Elizabeth
Chowning, 7 Sept 1771, William King sec.

Sydnor, William m. Rachell Davenport 16 Dec 1717
William Payne sec.

Sydnor, William m. Catherine Taylor 1 Mar 1724/5
Thomas Edwards sec.

Sydnor, William m. Margaret S. Brent 10 Mar 1813
John Ingram sec.

Sydnor, William m. Mary Kirk, dau. William Kirk
11 Feb 1817, James Kirk sec.

Tackleson, Taekle m. Elizabeth George, sister of
William George, 16 Dec 1793, William George
sec.

Taff, John m. Elizabeth Dodson 26 Dec 1808, George
Ashburne sec.

Tally, Champion m. Nancy C. Cornish 2 Sept 1806,
Robert D. Palmer sec.

Tally, Daniel J. m. Polly Palmer 30 Sept 1833,
Thomas Palmer sec.

Talley, George m. Nancy Pitman 18 Jan 1796, Robert
Brooke sec.

Talley, George m. Lucy Selvey 10 Dec 1827, Isaac
Cundiff sec.

Tally, James m. Nancy Robinson 1 Jan 1816, James
Robinson sec.

Tally, James m. Virginia Stimson 16 Dec 1836
George Tallay sec.

Tally, Johohn, Jr. m. Jemimah Webb 7 Nov 1796, Lot
Palmer sec.

Tally, Thomas J. m. Hannah Webb 22 Mar 1796
Charles Leland sec.

Talley, John m. Mary Chilton 10 June 1828, Isaac
Cundiff sec.

Tankard, John W. m. Susan W. Taylor, dau. Thorowgood
Taylor, 10 June 1839, William T. Dalby sec.

Tapscott, Edney m. Mary Waugh 15 Feb 1762, James
Tapscott sec.

Tapscott, Henry m. Mary Shearman 11 Feb 1758
Martin Shearman sec.

Tapscott, Henry m. Sarah Yopp 19 Feb 1810, William
Brown sec.

Tapscott, Henry m. Ailcy Cundiff 1 July 1829
Warner Lunsford sec.

Tapscott, John m. Mary Spilman 8 Sept 1786, John
Sullivant sec.

Tapscott, Joseph m. Elizabeth T. Hutchings 19 Feb
1829, Isaac Brent sec.

Tapscott, Joseph m. Mary M. Mitchell, dau. George
M. Mitchell, 15 Oct 1832, Samuel Gresham sec.

Tapscott, Joseph m. Margaret C. Doggett 19 Feb
1835 Elias B. Edmonds sec.

Tapscott, Martin m. Mary Rowand 16 June 1785,Joseph
      Shearman sec.
Tapscott, Rawleigh m. Ann Shearman -- 1783, Joseph
      Shearman sec.
Tapscott, Richard m. Frances George, dau. Frances
      George, 14 Aug 1789, John Rogers, Jr. sec.
Tapscott, Robert m. Olivia Degges 11 Sept 1832
      Robert T. Dunaway sec.
Tarkelson, Tarkel m. Margaret Thatcher 3 June 1797
      George P. Oliver sec.
Taylor, Isaac m. Elizabeth Carter 9 Aug 1785
      Elijah Purcifull sec.
Taylor, Thomas m. Eve Ball dau. James Ball, 12
      Dec 1741, Thomas Edwards sec.
Tayloe, Thomas m. Lucy Boyd 30 Nov 1840,Thomas C.
      Callahan sec.
Thatcher, George m. Milly Haydon 10 Feb 1798,John
      Edwards sec.
Thomas, Griffin E. m. Nancy Webb 4 Jan 1831,Ewell
      Webb sec.
Thomas, John m. Mary Gains 26 Dec 1826, William C.
      Callahan sec.
Thomas, John W. m. Margaret Seebry 25 Dec 1828
      Benjamin Waddy sec.
Thomas, Rodham m. Elizabeth Wilkerson 15 July 1784
      Samuel Dunaway sec.
Thomas, Vincent m. Sukey Bean 24 May 1808, Thomas
      Dodson sec.
Thomas, Vincent m. Sally Beane 1 Feb 1821, George
      Thomas sec.
Thomas, Washington m. Mary Oliver 11 Dec 1834
      James Pinn sec.
Thomson, Leroy m. Harriet Rich dau. Eppa Rich, 29
      Oct 1839, Sephus Newman sec.
Thrift, John F. m. Eliza Douglass 4 June 1833,
      John Thrift sec.
Thrift, Thomas m. Judith Thomas 4 June 1835 Edward
      Payne sec.
Thrift, Thomas m. Margaret Ann Doggett 27 Nov 1841
      William Doggett sec.
Thrift, John F. m. Ann E. Bloxom 22 Dec 1846
      Braxton Kirkham sec.
Thrall,John m. Ellen George 2 Feb 1780, John James
      sec.
Thrall, John m. Judith Clarke 17 Dec 1810, George
      Pitman sec.
Thrall, James m. Ann Carpenter 28 Oct 1835,William
      C. Carpenter sec.

Thrall, Thomas m. Rebecca M. George 1 Feb 1809
George Arms sec.

Thrailkill, Lindsey m. Ann Stonum 20 Jan 1790
Phillip Warwick sec.

Tibbes, Foushee G. m. Sarah Downman 30 Sept 1823
George W. Downman sec.

Ticer, Samuel m. Alice Riveer 6 Dec 1826, James
Riveer sec.

Timberlake, Francis m. Judith Lawson 9 Mar 1730
Hugh Brent sec.

Toby, Thomas W. m. Isabella Hall 26 Nov 1846
Robert T. Dunaway sec.

Toleman, John m. Susanna Williams 15 Dec 1808, Enoch
George sec.

Towell, Mark m. Ann Hunton 5 Jan 1782, William
Hinton sec.

Towell, Richard m. Sally Hinton 24 Sept 1811
James B. Galloway sec.

Towell, Capt. Thomas m. Ann Currell Lee, dau.
Thomas Lee, 15 Mar 1808, David Buchan sec.

Towles, Henry m. Judith Haynes 19 May 1768
Merryman Payne sec.

Towles, Henry, Jr. m. Alice Chilton 21 May 1795
William Chowning sec.

Towles, James m. Felicia Chowning 8 Oct 1807, John
Chowning sec.

Towles, James S. m. Sarah L. Towles 13 Aug 1833
William H. Towles sec.

Towles, John m. Sophronia E. Chowning 30 July 1835
Benjamin M. Walker sec.

Towles, Oliver m. Margaret Yerby, only dau. of
William Yerby, 14 June 1809, William Yerby sec.

Towles, Oliver m. Louisa C. George 25 Dec 1843,
George H. Webb sec.

Towles, Portens m. Frances Towles 18 Feb 1802,
Stokely Towles sec.

Towles, Stokely m. Elizabeth Martin dau. Katherine
Brent, 12 Mar 1736/7, James Brent sec.

Towles, Stokely m. Mary W. Ball 21 Jan 1799, James
Towles sec.

Towles, Thomas m. Kitturah George 9 Sept 1822
William H. Towles sec.

Towles, William P. m. Lucy K. Degge 8 Mar 1815
James Towles sec.

Travers, William m. Chloe Ingram dau. Mary Ingram
18 Oct 1818, Archibald Hinton sec.

Treacle, Dempsey, son of Richard Treacle, m.
Martha Wheeler, wid. 10 Oct 1805, James
Towles sec.

Treakle, Dempsey m. Mary Ashbourne 17 Apr 1838, James
    Treakle sec.
Treakle, James m. Louisa B. Bridgeman 15 Oct 1836
    Thomas Spriggs sec.
Treakle, James m. Mary Ann Yerby 20 Apr 1846, Cyrus
    Swanson sec.
Treakle, James W. M. Mary Dameron 15 July 1848
    William Flowers sec.
Treakle, John S. m. Frances Hutchinson 13 June
    1828, Thomas James sec.
Treacle, John G. m. Elizabeth Hutchinson 16 Dec
    1829, Thomas James sec.
Treakle, John K. m. Polly Hughlett 25 Apr 1844
    Edward Payne sec.
Treekle, Samuel m. Judith Williams 4 Nov 1815
    Dempsey Treakle sec.
Treacke, William m. Judith Bottoms 23 Dec 1823
    Samuel Treacle sec.
Treakle, William m. Elizabeth B. Yerby 15 May
    1837, Isaac Pitman sec.
Treakle, William T. m. Elizabeth Gains 29 July
    1841, John Alford sec.
Trott, Benjamin m. Clary P. Doggett 22 Jan 1834
    William Brown sec.
Tuck, Joseph m. Patsy Bradberry 11 Feb. 1811
    James Bradberry sec.
Tucker, St. George, of the City of Williamsburg,
    m. Lelia Carter, wid. 3 Oct 1791,
    Elizabeth Currie sec.
Turner, Benjamin m. Elizabeth Henderson 19 July
    1845, Thomas A. Sorrel sec.

Vanlandingham, George m. Elizabeth W. Cockarell
    15 Jan 1824, Charles Lewis sec.
Vanlandingham, Mandrid m. Elizabeth Dozier 17
    June 1844, William Walker sec.
Van Ness, Isaac m. Mary L. Hunt 29 Apr 1841
    William B. Hunt sec.
Vanness, Julius B. m. Ann S. Forrester 9 ----
    1837, Warren M. C. George sec.
Vaughn, John m. Chloe Hubbard 1 Apr 1805
    Edward Pinckard sec.
Veney, Simon m. Betsey Laws 5 May 1818, Thomas
    G. Robertson sec.
Veny, Robert m. Buky Wadkins 24 Mar 1834, Leroy
    Lewin sec.
Viena, Richard m. Judith Viena 16 June 1831
    Cyrus Wicken & John Pinn sec.

Vowel, Valentine H. m. Elizabeth L. James 9 Jan
1827, Thomas Armstrong sec.

Waddey, Benjamin, Jr. m. Margaret Payne 1 Dec.1766
William Chilton sec.
Waddey, Benjamin m. Janette P. Edmonds 27 Nov 1817
James Brent sec.
Waddy, George m. Elizabeth Maxwell 7 Jan 1796
Thomas W. Ingram sec.
Waddy, James m. Hannah Edwards, wid. 1 Oct 1770
Peter Miller sec.
Waddy, Jesse m. Mary Taylor 29 Oct 1779, Thomas
Dameron sec.
Waddey, John m. Delia Yerby 20 Sept 1819, Walter
B. Waddy sec.
Waddel, James m. Mary Gordon, dau. James Gordon,
7 Oct 1767, Edney Tapscott sec.
Waddel, Nathaniel m. Mary Smith Gordon, dau.
James Gordon, 4 June 1793, James Gordon
Waddel sec.
Waide, Robert C. m. Alice M. George 23 Dec 1801
Enock George sec.
Wall, John R. m. Janett James 15 June 1829,Morris
Emanuel sec.
Wall, Richard m. Nancy M. Newby, dau. William
Newby, 28 Jan 1815, Edward Oldham sec.
Wall, Samuel m. Ellen Dameron 20 Jan 1814,Thomas
B. Oliver sec.
Wallace, James m. Grace Walker 20 July 1780,Jesse
Waddy sec.
Wale, Lawson m. Winifred Spriggs 15 May 1783,
Moses Hesten sec.
Walker, Baldwin m. Sarah Chilton 22 Dec 1824,John
T. Degges,Jr. sec.
Walker, Benjamin M. m. Lucy Simmons 2 Jan 1822
Spencer George sec.
Walker, George S. m. Elener H. Forester 15 Mar
1841, Thaddeus Forester sec.
Walker, John m. Leanna Treacle 24 Feb 1820,Samuel
Treacle sec.
Walker, John m. Betsy Whealer 15 Jan 1823 ,Samuel
Treacle sec.
Walker, Joseph m. Jane Newby 5 Jan. 1796, James
Newby sec.
Walker, Joseph m. Sally G. Schofield 16 Nov 1807
William Kirk sec.
Walker, Joseph m. Mary G. Chilton 27 Mar 1843
Robert Edmonds sec.

Walker, Presley m. Salley K. Cottral 20 Feb 1815
    Thomas Currell sec.
Walker, Presley m. Ann Jefferson 9 May 1827, Isaac
    Currell sec.
Walker, Robert m. Sary Ann Sebree 17 Apr 1777
    Moses George sec.
Walker, Thomas C. m. Mary C. George 4 Dec 1837
    Robert H. Tapscott sec.
Walker, William m. Harriet Gundra 15 July 1848
    Thomas D. Palmer sec.
Warwick, Benjamin m. Charlotte George 25 Jan 1792
    John Wilder sec.
Warwick, James m. Ann Deselve 23 Nov 1820,
    Benjamin Palmer sec.
Warwick, James m. Polly Thrift 7 May 1825, John
    Thrift sec.
Warwick, John m. Mary Arms 9 June 1835, Richard
    F. Bryant
Warwick, Phillip m. Ann Stott, dau. Elizabeth
    Stott, 4 Sept 1787, John Dunaway sec.
Warwick, Philip m. Nancy Stott 22 Feb 1825
    William C. Carpenter sec.
Warwick, Thomas m. Jane Brown 9 Jan 1817
    William Brown sec.
Warwick, William m. Eleanor Garner, wid. of
    William Garner, 15 Sept 1794, George
    Warwick sec.
Warwick, William m. Elizabeth Ashbourn 28 May
    1822, William Yerby sec.
Warrick, George m. Ann Edney George 31 July
    1797, Benjamin Warrick sec.
Wornam, Charles m. Julia A. Webb 26 Dec 1833
    Jesse Hubbard sec.
Wornham, Thomas H. m. Elizabeth Sebry 10 Jan
    1833, William George sec.
Wornom, Thomas m. Lucy Hubbard 19 Dec 1808
    John George sec.
Wornum, Thomas m. Lucy Kirkham, dau. John
    Kirkham, 19 Jan 1829, Jesse Hubbard sec.
Watts, Ewell m. Rebecca Carter 5 Oct 1831
    Joseph Webb sec.
Watts, John m. Bridget Payne 25 Jan 1797
    Edward Payne sec.
Watts, John E. m. Ann Kellam 6 June 1826
    Thomas M. Owens sec.
Wats, Spencer m. Betsy Butler - Consent dated
    30 Mar. 1801 - Not signed
Waters, Thomas L. m. Ann L. Lowell 6 Apr 1830
    Robert Smither sec.

Waters, William of Somersett County, Maryland, m.
Augusteen C. Humphries 10 Dec 1829, Robert
Smither sec.

Wayman, John m. Lucinda Blakemore 11 Sept 1805
Edward Blakemore sec.

Weaver, Henry m. Jenny Weaver 28 Nov 1811, Andrew
Chilton sec.

Weaver, John m. Dorcus Bell 10 June 1789, Elijah
Weaver sec.

Weaver, Moses m. Janetta Smith 31 Dec 1816, James
Brent sec.

Weaver, Moses m. Ahrella Thornton 7 Sept 1844
Robert T. Dunaway sec.

Weaver, Thomas m. Elizabeth Lawes 7 July 1794
Elijah Weaver sec.

Weaver, Thomas m. Elizabeth Dunaway, dau.
Elizabeth Dunaway, 7 Dec 1839, Overton
Nickcn sec.

Webb, Charles m. Mary Sullivant, wid. 6 June 1795
Richard Lee sec.

Webb, Charles m. Sally Overstreet 30 May 1804

Webb, George m. Alice Tapscott 23 Dec 1808,
William Kelly sec.

Webb, George m. Polly L. Neale 15 Mar 1820, James
Brent sec.

Webb, James m. Mary Holder 6 Mar 1769, Richard
Selden sec.

Webb, James R. m. Mary C. Ingram 24 Dec 1845
George H. Webb sec.

Webb, Joseph m. Priscilla Doggett 5 June 1817
Robert D. Palmer sec.

Webb, James m. Rebecka Percifull 20 Dec 1819, John
Sampson sec.

Webb, Joseph m. Katherine Dunaway 28 July, 1835
Daniel Talley sec.

Webb, Joseph m. Eliza Ann Brown 16 Feb 1841, John
Brown sec.

Webb, Joseph m. Elizabeth Thomas, dau. Susanna
Thomas, 20 Dec 1844, George W. Sampson sec.

Webb, Thomas m. Judith Baisey 30 Sept 1786,
Samuel Sutton sec.

Webb, Thomas m. Molly Boatman 16 Feb 1795, William
Boatman sec.

Webb, Thomas m. Mary Tally 4 Feb 1797, John Tally
sec.

Webb, William m. Patty Hill, 21 Sept 1784, William
Hunt sec.

Weblin, William, Jr. m. Sarah Beavens 17 Mar 1788
    John Newby sec.
West, James m. Huldah Hammond 15 Feb 1841, Lewis
    Hammond sec.
West, James m. Elizabeth Hammond 22 Dec 1848, James
    S. George sec.
West, Joseph m. Betsey Chitwood 22 Nov 1802,
    Bartley Overstreet sec.
West, Joseph m. Betsey Toleman 16 Dec 1816, William
    George sec.
West, Robert, of Richmond County, m. Margaret
    Buckles, 20 June, 1735, Hugh Brent sec.
Wessels, Custis m. Nancy Nayson 17 Nov 1842, Jesse
    Duncan sec.
Wharton, Joseph m. Ann Edmunds, dau. Elias Edmunds
    4 June 1737, Robert Edmunds sec.
Wheeler, Moses m. Martha Williams, dau. Peter
    Williams, 30 May 1799, Peter Williams sec.
White, Griffin m. Polly Demeritt 31 Dec 1793
    William Carpenter sec.
White, Isaac m. Mary Ann Ewell 11 Oct 1727, William
    Ballendine sec.
Wilder, George m. Sukey Davis 31 Jan 1786, William
    Davis sec.
Wilder, Jonathan m. Mary Overstreet 18 Mar 1794
    Bartlet Overstreet sec.
Wilder, John m. Lucy Webb 8 May 1793, Jonathan
    Wilder sec.
Wilder, Michael m. Ann Carter 18 May 1780, Robert
    Chinn sec.
Wilder, Michael m. Mary McCally 27 Nov 1793
    William Stewart Wilder sec.
Wilder, Michael, Jr. m. Nancy Hammonds, dau. Nancy
    Hammonds, 15 June 1824, Thomas James sec.
Wilder, Newman m. Nancy George 17 -- 1794, John
    Longworth, Jr. sec.
Wilder, Spencer m. Sally Yopp 30 May 1789, Charles
    Hubbard sec.
Wilder, William m. Sally Davis 18 May 1786, Jesse
    Wilder sec.
Wilcox, James m. Nancy Hill 26 Jan 1803, John
    Cornelious sec.
Wilson, Cyrus m. Olivia Stott 21 Dec 1814, James
    Towles sec.
Wilson, James E. m. Elizabeth H. Connolly 16 Apr
    Cyrus Riveer sec.
Wilson, William m. Molly Taylor Schofield 19 Jan
    1791, John Fendla, Jr. sec.

Williams, James C. m. Lucy Hutchings 29 Nov 1827
William Scrimger sec.

Williams, John m. Molley Balley 16 Oct 1792 Richard
Mitchell sec.

Williams, John m. Sarah Mason 18 Sept 1798, John
Atkins sec.

Williams, Peter m. Alcy Connolly, dau. Patrick
Connolly, 25 Sept 1792, James Connolly sec.

Williams, Peter m. Leannah Doggett, 6 Jan 1835
James C. Williams sec.

Williams, Peter m. Mary Ann Beane 21 Nov 1843
Johnson Beane sec.

Williams, William m. Sarah Cornelious 17 Dec 1798
Alexander Elliott sec.

Winstead, Lucius S. m. Elizabeth A. Pitman 3 Oct
1836, Cyrus Riveer sec.

Wood, Holland m. Jane Haw 15 Oct 1821, Hiram
Carpenter sec.

Wood, Holland m. Sally Wood 14 Jan 1834, John
Hurst sec.

Wood, John m. Janetta Hutchings 17 Sept 1821, John
Hutchings sec.

Wood, Samuel m. Anna Rich 28 Dec 1831, John Wood
sec.

Wood, Thomas m. Sally Bee 20 Jan 1813, Charles
Wood sec.

Wood, Thomas m. Lucy Cox, dau. Patty Cox, 30 May
1833, John Hurst sec.

Wooddy, John m. Ann N. Herron 23 Dec 1828, George
C. Newgent sec.

Woody, Thomas m. Alcinda Kid 21 Feb 1878, James
Towles sec.

Woodson, John, of Goochland County, m. Mary
Miller 10 Aug. 1731, William Miller sec.

Wormely, John, of Middlesex County m. Ann Taylor,
dau. of William Taylor, 20 June 1746,
Thomas Edwards the elder sec.

Wormeley, John m. Fanny Bond 19 Aug 1784, John
Doggett sec.

Wren, William m. Joannah George 17 May 1756
William James sec.

Wyatt, John m. Mary Harwood Currell 24 Dec. 1783
Epp[a]: Lawson sec.

Yerby, Charles J. m. Sally Chilton, dau. Judith
Chilton, 21 Feb 1814, W. T. Yerby sec.

Yerby, Charles m. Jane Pedsley Towell, dau. Mark
Towell, 19 June 1815, William T. Yerby sec.

Yerby, Charles H. m. Margaret J. George dau. Zamoth
George, 7 Dec 1842, Isaac Currell sec.

Yerby, Ellyson m. Hannah Meredith 7 Apr 1823
Charles Taylor sec.

Yerby, George W. m. Elizabeth Meredith 17 Oct 1782
William Gibson sec.

Yerby, James T. m. Catherine Basye 17 Mar 1835
Robert T. Dunaway sec.

Yerby, Richard m. Judith George 16 Feb 1786, Elijah
Percifull sec.

Yerby, Thomas m. Hannah Dogget 22 Feb 1717/18
------ Doggott sec. (badly damaged)

Yerby, William m. Frances McTire, dau. Robert
McTire, 17 Apr 1753, James Kirk sec.

Yerby, William m. Lida Shore 19 May 1819, Thomas
Schofield sec.

Yerby, William m. Harriott Beane dau. Opie Beane
14 Jan 1824, Opie Beane sec.

Yerby, William m. Elizabeth B. Wilson 7 Mar 1827
Elias & James Fendla sec.

Yerby, William m. Cordelia M. Chilton 23 Feb 1729
Fauntleroy N. Chilton sec.

Yopp, Samuel m. Mary Simmons, dau. Elizabeth
Simmons, 3 July 1754, William Shelton sec.

Yopp, Samuel m. Molly Doggett 25 Apr 1782
Jedithen Brent sec.

	Page
Ball, Sarah	66
Ball, Sarah	26
Ball, Sarah	43
Ball, Sarah	27
Balley, Molley	80
Ballind---, --an--	53
Barker, Catherine	3
Barnet, Elizabeth S. B.	20
Barnett, Milly	16
Barnett, Dolly	37
Barnes, Mary Jane	13
Barrick, Catherine	10
Barrick, Elizabeth	15
Barrick, Nancy P.	21
Barrick, Sarah D.	29
Barrock, Elizabeth	47
Basye, Catherine	81
Basye, Nancy	53
Basye, Polly	17
Baylie, Hannah	61
Beane, Ann C.	56
Beane, Catherine	4
Beane, Charlotte T.	22
Beane, Harriott	81
Beane, Jane O.	39
Beane, Judith	15
Beane, Leanna	13
Beane, Lidda R.	60
Beane, Margaret Ann	41
Beane, Mary B.	4
Beane, Mary Ann	80
Beane, Milly	41
Bean, Molly	48
Beane, Nancy	5
Beane, Polly	10
Beane, Sally	73
Bean, Sukey	73

	Page
Beale, Ailcey O.	25
Beavens, Sarah	79
Bell, Ann	43
Bell, Betty	59
Bell, Betsey	43
Bell, Darkey	48
Bell, Dorcus	78
Bell, Mary	43
Bell, Margaret	54
Bell, Nancy	1
Bee, Sally	80
Bennet, Mary	49
Bertrand, Mary Ann	34
Berryman, Frances B.	33
Berryman, Martha	26
Berryman, Sally	40
Billings, Mary	59
Biscoe, Elizabeth L.	4
Biscoe, Mary C.	41
Biscoe, Nancy	40
Biscoe, Polly	41
Blade, Ellen	40
Blakesby, Frances	11
Blakey, Frances	56
Bland, Nancy	25
Blackmore, Elizabeth	43
Blackmore, Elizabeth R.	10
Blackmore, Hannah	27
Blakemore, Bridget	58
Blakemore, Hannah	5
Blakemore, Lilly T.	53
Blakemore, Lucinda	78
Blakemore, Mary J.	56

	Page			Page
Blakemore, Molly	41	Brent, Elizabeth H.		61
Blakemore, Nancy	66	Brent, Ellinor		69
		Brent, Fanny		8
Bloxom, Ann E.	73	Brent, Frances		12
		Brent, Frances		51
Boatman, Elizabeth	39	Brent, Hannah		46
Boatman, Harriet J.	31	Brent, Jane Swan		56
Boatman, Margaret Ann	68	Brent, Jane Newton		63
Boatman, Molly	78	Brent, Judith		2
		Brent, Judith N.		47
Boid, Frankey	65	Brent, Katherine, Jr.		11
		Brent, Lettice L.		63
Boling, Winifred	43	Brent, Lucinda		40
		Brent, Lucy		18
Bond, Fanny	80	Brent, Lucy		8
Bond, Morning	43	Brent, Mary E. L.		37
		Brent, Margaret		63
Boothe, Juliet C.	4	Brent, Margaret S.		72
		Brent, Molly		7
Bottoms, Elizabeth	16	Brent, Polly		21
Bottoms, Judith	75	Brent, Priscilla		70
Bottoms, Lucy	27	Brent, Sally		46
		Brent, Salley N.		42
Bourke, Rebecca	57	Brent, Sarah		46
		Brent, Sarah		14
Boyd, Lucy	73	Brent, Sarah		68
Boyd, Winifred	35	Brent, Susey		28
		Brent, Susanna		31
Bradberry, Patsy	75			
		Brinnin, Bridget		6
Branan, Caty	54			
		Bridgeman, Louisa B.		75
Branberry, Elizabeth	59			
		Bridgford, Judith		18
Brent, Ann S.	33			
Brent, Ann N.	41	Briscoe, Lyddy		60
Brent, Ann S.	8			
Brent, Ann S.	51	Brounley, Kitty Ann		21
Brent, Betty	60			
Brent, Catherine	58	Brown, Amanda		17
Brent, Catherine	64	Brown, Eliza Ann		78
Brent, Catherine L.	63	Brown, Elizabeth		20
Brent, Charlotte	70	Brown, Esther		2
Brent, Elizabeth	42	Brown, Harriett		11
Brent, Elizabeth	52	Brown, Jane		77
Brent, Elizabeth	8	Brown, Kitty		62
Brent, Eliza L.	50	Brown, Mary Ann		34

		Page			Page
Currie,	Eliza H. A	71	Davenport,	Rachell	71
Currie,	Frances Hill	1	Davenport,	Rachel	1
Currie,	Jane	4	Davenport,	Sally	57
Curril,	Elizabeth F	23	Davis,	Alcy	70
			Davis,	Annie	45
Currell,	Ann	53	Davis,	Betsey Johnson	14
Currell,	Catherine	58	Davis,	Delia G.	66
Currell,	Ellinor	59	Davis,	Dorothy	25
Currell,	Elizabeth	48	Davis,	Elizabeth	13
Currell,	Elizabeth F.	28	Davis,	Elizabeth	
Currell,	Elizabeth	47		Rivers	58
Currell,	Elizabeth H.	10	Davis,	Elizabeth	44
Currell,	Elizabeth H.	17	Davis,	Frances	6
Currell,	Elizabeth	42	Davis,	Hagar	62
Currell,	Judith A.	65	Davis,	Judah	14
Currell,	Lucy	29	Davis,	Judith	26
Currell,	Mary	40	Davis,	Judith	22
Currell,	Mary Harwood	80	Davis,	Milley	51
Currell,	Mary S.	30	Davis,	Nancy	62
Currell,	Molly	36	Davis,	Nancy	51
Currell,	Nancy C.	32	Davis,	Parmelia	66
Currell,	Sally	18	Davis,	Polly P.	56
Currell,	Sally B.	61	Davis,	Sally	79
Currell,	Sally S.	48	Davis,	Sally	26
Currell,	Sarah Ann	59	Davis,	Sukey	79
			Davis,	Thomazin	51
Dameron,	Barbary	69			
Dameron,	Elizabeth	16	Day,	Sally	24
Dameron,	Elizabeth	35			
Dameron,	Elizabeth L.	8	Deggs,	Ann	7
Dameron,	Ellen	76			
Dameron,	Judith Barret	61	Degge,	Catherine C.	52
Dameron,	Mary Ann	7	Degge,	Lucy K.	74
Dameron,	Mary	75	Degge,	Mary	6
Dameron,	Margaret L.	10	Degge,	Mary	30
Dameron,	Sarah	19			
			Degges,	Amelia	21
Danson,	Ann C.	44	Degges,	Dolly	52
			Degges,	Dorothy L	11
Darby,	Judith	49	Degges,	Olivia	73
Daugherty,	Matilda P.	21	Demeratt,	Nancy	
				Branham	23
Davenport,	Ann	24	Demeritt,	Polly	79
Davenport,	Eliza	50			
Davenport,	Elizabeth H	55	Denny,	Lucy	47
Davenport,	Judith	37			

	Page		Page
Deselve, Ann	77	Doggett, Sarah	22
DeSelvey, Alice	58	Doggett, Winifred	53
Digges, Mary Tunstall	47	Douglass, Eliza	73
Dillard, Mary	51	Downing, Mary	56
Dillard, Martha	12		
		Downman, Fidelia	2
Dinns? --------	42	Downman, Frances	53
		Downman, Frances	33
Dix, Catherine E.	38	Downman, Harriot	
		. Jane	23
Dobyns, Barbara	32	Downman, Jane E.	27
Dobyns, Matilda C.	30	Downman, Margaret	53
		Downman, Millan	3
Dodson, Elizabeth	72	Downman, Million E.	14
Dodson, Judith	1	Downman, Olivia	13
Dodson, Nancy	20	Downman, Priscilla	23
Dodson, Peggy	7	Downman, Priscilla	7
Dodson, Polly	60	Downman, Sarah	74
Doggett, Ann	16	Dozier, Elizabeth	75
Doggett, Ann	40		
Doggett, Ann M.	49	Dudley, Peggy	66
Doggett, Betty	12		
Dogget, Betty	19	Dunton, Catherine	35
Doggett, Betsey	22		
Doggett, Clary P	75	Dunaway, Asksah	14
Doggett, Elizabeth	12	Dunaway, Caty	26
Doggett, Elizabeth A	69	Dunaway, Catherine	22
Doggett, Emily M.	60	Dunaway, Eliza	24
Doggett, Hannah	81	Dunaway, Elizabeth	54
Doggett, Hannah	37	Dunaway, Elizabeth	78
Doggett, Harriott	13	Dunaway, Elizabeth	71
Doggett, Joanna	70	Dunnaway, Fanny	64
Doggett, Judith	30	Dunaway, Judith	56
Doggett, Leannah	80	Dunaway, Katherine	78
Doggett, Lucy	36	Dunaway, Kitty Ann	55
Doggett, Mary Ann	22	Dunaway, Lucy	3
Doggett, Mary Ann	37	Dunaway, Mary	
Doggett, Margaret C.	72	Chowning	2
Doggett, Margaret Ann	73	Dunaway, Margaret	6
Doggett, Molly	81	Dunaway, Margaret	58
Doggett, Molly	50	Dunaway, Milly	12
Doggett, Patsy P.	28	Dunaway, Nancy	40
Doggett, Polly Smith	58	Dunaway, Nancy	9
Doggett, Priscilla	45		
Doggett, Priscilla	78	Dye, Catherine	15

	Page		Page
James, Elizabeth	31	Keeling, Betsy	13
James, Elizabeth	45		
James, Elizabeth	49	Kelly, Letty	47
James, Elizabeth L.	76	Kelley, Sarah	10
James, Elizabeth	18		
James, Elizabeth M. R.	67	Kellam, Ann	77
James, Frances	18	Kellum, Mary E.	41
James, Janett	76		
James, Mary	18	Kemm, Lucy	18
James, Mary	34	Kemm, Roxey	60
James, Mary K.	32	Kemm, Susan	68
James, Mary P.	49		
James, Margaret	60	Kemp, Cretia	17
James, Margaret	51		
James, Polly B.	39	Kent, Ann	15
James, Polley B.	42	Kent, Catherine	38
James, Rebecca M.	51	Kent, Elizabeth	17
James, Rebecca M.	41	Kent, Elizabeth S.	17
James, Sally	16	Kent, Frances	11
James, Sarah	56	Kent, Jane W.	25
James, Sarah B.	51	Kent, Jemima	17
		Kent, Nancy	67
Jarrett, Fanny	10	Kent, Nancy	38
		Kent, Polly S.	18
Jeff, Mary Ann	28	Kent, Priscilla	9
		Kent, Salley	45
Jefferson, Ann	77	Kent, Winny	65
Jefferson, Elizabeth	31		
		Kenner, Mary	65
Jesper, Josephine T.	21		
		Kern, Betty	50
Johnson, Martha Ann	41	Kernn, Betsey	64
Johnson, Rosetta	50		
		Kester, Henrietta B.	52
Jones, Anne	27		
Jones, Athaliah A.	40	Kesterson, Felicia	34
Jones, Behethelem	54		
Jones, Hannah	62	Kid, Alcinda	80
Jones, Mary D.	11	Kidd, Louisa A. C.	32
Jones, Maria L.	19		
Jones, Margaret	5	King, Catherine	21
Jones, Nancy	27	King, Judith	8
Jones, Patty	1	King, Judith	8
Jones, Rhoda	43	King, Mary	18
Jones, Sally	51	King, Winifred	13
Jones, Sally	42		
		Kirk, Anne	54
Jopes, Molly P.	59	Kirk, Ann Y.	25

106

www.ingramcontent.com/pod-product-compliance
Lightning Source LLC
Chambersburg PA
CBHW021836020426

42334CB00014B/656